Wilderness Voices

by Al Youmans

A voice crying in the wilderness (John 1:23)

Copyright © 2016
ISBN:1540442896

Table of Contents

Foreword
Prospective

Written language and critical thinking have always been challenged by the ongoing social tension between respect and repression.

Freedom of speech allows, and requires, individual readers to make their own responsible determination as to the relevance and meaning of the written word.

Regardless of the motivation or intentions of such initiatives as political correctness, cultural sensitivity, religious dogma or state security, only the free exchange of all ideas will ultimately establish the true meaning and understanding of the words we use.

The multiple access, instantaneous, electronic communications technology increasingly competes with the written word for our attention by providing immediate individual and social engagement with minimal effort.

Only experience will determine whether the bigger threat to the written word is political manipulation, lack of cultural attention or ease of technical usage.

Whether the encroaching wilderness of distraction and distortion is political, cultural or technical in nature.

§

While fiction pursues entertainment, reality demands acknowledgement.

3

A Brief Glossary

Congress shall make no law ... abridging the freedom of speech (1st Amendment)

A bridge – A structure for providing passage over an obstacle

Abridge – To lessen the strength of a right

Political Correctness:
- *Structuring words to provide passage over obstinate sensibilities*
- *Substitute terms to lessen the strength of accurate words*
- *An abstract terminology seeking respect but achieving absurdity*

Culture – What we as a society choose to do; or not do

Denial – Refusing to accept an unpopular truth

Acceptance – Corresponding with reality

Metaphor – A figure of speech providing a novel yet illuminating comparison

Satire – A literary attempt to illuminate distortion through a subtle blend of wit and metaphor

*Remember – It's called the Bill of Rights;
Not Lefts.*

The Spark

It is estimated humans began writing sometime between 7,000 and 30,000 years ago. We can only speculate how the written word was first developed and used...

It came to Kort from an unknown place.

He wasn't even looking for it.

The thought...the idea...the picture...the sound...the thing...

Once it appeared, it seemed like it had always been there.

Kort wondered if anyone else had seen this before. How could somebody not see this? It seemed so common. It seemed so straight forward.

Should he say something to the others? Would they think him foolish for asking them about this? Would they laugh at him for stating the obvious? Would they mock his ignorance? Would they become angry at his disrespect?

Worse yet, what if they didn't understand? Their potential blank looks could be more cutting than any rejection or mockery or physical punishment.

However, it seemed so clear. It seemed so natural. It seemed so normal.

Kort wants to tell somebody. He needs to show somebody. It could benefit him by raising his importance in the eyes of the others. He could help others to use it.

If the truth be known, it could benefit all in his group by its use. It could give them an advantage above the other bands they come into contact with in their travels and in their trade.

However, why should his group listen to Kort? He had done nothing noteworthy in the group before this. Others have higher positions. Others have more experience. Others are listened to for their ideas and looked to for their direction.

Yet, Kort feels this should be known. He feels this should be shared. He feels it should be used.

It must be known. It will be known. He will tell the others. But Kort needs to practice it so he can better show them its use and value.

§

Kort awoke the next morning and it was still there.

In fact, it was more there today than it was yesterday. He can't wait to go back to the stream to start practicing with it.

However, Kort has family tasks he needs to complete before he can get away to practice it.

Kort completes his tasks as quickly as possible. Even though these were common things that he had done many times, Kort finds it difficult to keep his mind on doing them.

It dawns on him that such tasks could be made easier by the use of it. And if his tasks can be made better, others' work can also be made better. Such insight energizes Kort even more. He can't wait to get to the stream to practice.

Kort gets to the stream. He finds a smooth part of the bank. He has kept the same branch that he used yesterday. Though, it dawns on him another branch would work just as well.

He begins to practice. The birds are here again today. However, there's something different about them. There are more types of them. Yesterday there were sparrows and blackbirds. Today there are sparrows, blackbirds, finches and thrushes.

That's when it came to him yesterday. The birds not only look different. They make different sounds when they sing. The different sounds of the birds, as well as the different appearances of the birds, help him to remember the different birds. These differences help him and others know which birds are which. These differences cause everyone to use different words, when talking about the birds.

Kort uses the stick to make marks in the bank mud. A mark to show the sparrow...a different mark to show the finch...one for blackbirds...one for thrushes...

After Kort makes the marks, he can tell others about the different birds. About what they look like; about how they sound; about what the marks mean. More importantly, these marks would let everyone tell each other the words used for these birds.

And most importantly, these marks can tell everyone how to say these words.

§

Who does Kort tell first? Who does he show first? Should it be one person? Should it be the all group? Should it be someone in his family? Should it be one of his friends? Should it be one of the leaders?

He decides to tell his friend Tal first. He feels he can trust Tal. He can trust his friend to look at this with an open mind. He can trust Tal to give him honest feedback. He can trust Tal not to tell anyone else until Kort is ready to tell them.

The next day Kort takes Tal to the bank by the stream. Luckily there are plenty of birds there again.

Kort says he wants to show Tal something. His friend laughs in his good-natured way. Tal eagerly asks if there are any girls in the water nearby.

Kort smiles and tells Tal they're not that lucky today. However, Tal may see something that he will remember for a long time. Kort can see he has Tal's attention.

Kort asks his friend to identify one of the birds flying around the stream. Tal points to one of the birds and calls out "sparrow". Kort takes a stick and makes a mark in the mud. They repeat this process until his friend has identified all the different types of birds around the stream.

Kort shows Tal the different marks. Tal looks at him with a puzzled expression. Kort asks Tal to point out one of the marks. Tal does and Kort says "finch".

Kort asks Tal to point to another mark; Kort says "sparrow". Another mark; Kort says "blackbird". Another mark; Kort says "thrush". Kort notices Tal appears to be thinking deeply.

Kort then points to a sparrow and gives Tal the stick. Kort again points to the sparrow; says its name; and guides the stick in Tal's hand to make the mark. Astonishment crosses Tal's face.

Kort points to a thrush. Tal takes the stick; grabs Kort's hand; and has Kort help him make the mark. A broad smile begins on Tal's mouth.

Tal points to a blackbird. He calls it a blackbird. Tal takes the stick. He makes the mark. He looks at Kort. Kort nods his head. Tal breaks out into a long, loud laugh.

They spend the rest of the afternoon writing all the things they can identify around the stream. They even come up with separate marks for "Kort" and "Tal".

§

Kort and Tal talk about who they should tell next. Tal feels this is important enough to show to the Leader of their group.

Kort appreciates Tal's support. For seeing the value of this thing in itself; as well as its importance to the whole group.

However, Kort is concerned he should not show anyone else until he shows it to his family. At least Kort needs to show it to his mother and father. Tal understands and agrees. It is always important, in matters of respect, to keep your family in your confidence. Both also guess the Leader would ask Kort's parents about their knowledge and views of this discovery.

Kort brings his parents and Tal back to the stream the next day. Both Tal and Kort demonstrate it to them. For some reason, it takes more examples and repetitions for Kort's parents to understand. However, Kort can tell by their facial and verbal expressions when they see the wonder of his discovery.

Upon returning from the stream, they discuss how, and when, Kort should tell the Leader and the rest of the group about this. They decide to do this as quickly as possible. This seems important enough, and valuable enough, to share with the group immediately.

Kort's father goes to the Leader to make an appointment. The meeting with the Leader and the entire group is set for mid-morning of the next day. Kort's father explains to the Leader that they will need to meet around the stream.

Though curious, the Leader agrees to this meeting place. He asks a few questions of Kort's father but does not seem overly concerned when Kort's father only responds in generalities about group interest and group importance.

Soon, the rest of the group hears about the upcoming meeting. Many curiosity seekers stop by that night with many questions. Kort's father merely replies all will be revealed tomorrow.

§

The group meets at the stream at mid-morning. There are many questions and a noticeable air of anticipation. The Leader calls the group to order. He explains that Kort has a discovery that may be of great importance to all in the group.

Kort starts off by explaining this idea came to him all of a sudden. One second, nothing. The next, it was there. Like a spark that starts a fire.

Kort again uses the example of the birds; as it was with the birds all of it started. With each bird, Kort makes the separate mark. Kort then uses other examples from around the stream that he and Tal developed. For some reason, it takes longer and more examples before Kort can see the understanding and wonder spreading through the faces of the whole group.

Kort caps the demonstration off with the mark he makes for himself.

At this point a loud scream pierces the area around the stream. It comes from the Shaman of the group.

The Shaman accuses Kort of witchcraft. The Shaman charges Kort with using the spirits of the birds to create something unnatural; something wicked. He claims Kort has stolen the spirits of the other animals and plants around the stream in the form of the marks Kort drew in the bank. These marks are evil and will only bring bad luck and misfortune to the group.

The group becomes fearful. Kort's parents and Tal try to reassure the group. However, the group quickly shifts from fear to anger.

They push Kort's family and Tal aside.

They attack Kort.

Kort's last thought becomes darkness.

§

The stream flows gently. The birds fly and sing serenely around the stream.

Up on a hill away from the stream is a new grave. After the burial is completed, a friend lingers at the gravesite.

When all have left, Tal takes a branch and makes Kort's mark in the freshly turned soil.

Springing Philosophy

*Humor is akin to philosophy for they are both viewpoints
born of a larger perspective of life.*

Will Durant

The word "philosophy" comes from the Greek meaning
"love of wisdom". For many, this "love" seems to be a self-
pleasuring manipulation of words by philosophers to
achieve a satisfaction they alone seem to appreciate.

However philosophy can be understood, even appreciated,
by non-philosophers.

Two of my favorite philosophical quotes come from Daniel
Dennett and Ludwig Wittgenstein. As philosophers, they
were committed to the discipline. They also displayed a
certain sense of humor about the subject. This is
evidenced by the following two statements:

• "My refusal to play ball with my colleagues is deliberate,
since I view the standard philosophical terminology as
worse than useless – a major obstacle to progress since it
consists of so many errors." Daniel Dennett

• "Philosophy is a battle against the bewitchment of our
intelligence by means of language. The meaning of a word
is its use in the language." Ludwig Wittgenstein

Whether based on skepticism or sarcasm, both seem to be
telling other philosophers to "lighten up". In order for
philosophy to be understood, it must be useful; it must be
more "user-friendly".

Philosophy is the study of the questions connected with human existence, knowledge, values, reason and language. Philosophy is distinguished by its reliance on rational argument. Rational argument based on a systematic approach.

And here lies the difficulty of understanding most philosophers. After a while their reasoning gets lost in a haze of confusing explanations.

Philosophy needs to spring forth from this difficulty.

There may be a more fundamental reason why philosophy is not only misunderstood, but also avoided and criticized.

Human beings both feel and think. This combination, or "duality", is what makes us human.

This human duality is even more complicated because humans are evolved social beings. As such social beings we continually search for the means to live well together. Philosophy searches for these means; these meanings.

As philosophy has focused more on thinking (the head) than feeling (the heart), philosophers often come off as rather cold or insensitive.

Let's further define philosophy as the tension between external facts and internal feelings in the pursuit of truth and reality. Thinking balanced, and challenged, by feeling to discover the truth.

Historically, the "tree" of philosophical truth has grown through its interwoven "branches" of conscious discovery:
• Logic: Structured Thinking
• Ethics: Values in Action
• Aesthetics: Beauty
• Politics: Power
• Epistemology: The Origin, Process and Validity of Knowledge
• Metaphysics: The Search for the Ultimate, Fundamental Reality

Most people seem to more readily understand logic, ethics, aesthetics and politics. Epistemology and metaphysics are not as easily grasped. The difficulty with these last two terms lies largely in their unfamiliarity.

The basics of logic, ethics, aesthetics, politics, epistemology and metaphysics must be plainly known for philosophy to be understandable and useful. These basics are the "buds" on the philosophical "branches" which produce the "flowers" of philosophical appreciation.

The budding basics...

Metaphysics...
One of the classic problems of philosophy has been the "mind-body" duality. As far as we know, human beings uniquely experience self-awareness. Whether this is called consciousness, the self, or the soul, it has always intrigued philosophers.

The body is the physical, external existence of humans. The mind is the mysterious mental, internal essence of humans.

The objective viewpoint is observable by others. The subjective viewpoint is an internal perception accessible only by the individual. Both exist together.

Susan Blackmore suggests dualism (the idea that mind and body are separate) is always tempting because it fits so well with the way our consciousness feels. There is much disagreement between philosophers, scientists, artists, religious followers and others on the actual relationship.

The duality of mind and body is really the tension between thinking and feeling.

Epistemology…
Man's nature is to acquire knowledge by his own desire and actions. Nature is a system of cause and effect.

Epistemology is a term mostly used, even flaunted, by philosophers.

Bottom line epistemology is about knowledge:
• Where it comes from
• How it develops
• Why it's true

Knowledge is gained from learning.

Learning is revealed by experience and creativity.

Innovation is the useful application of creativity.

Cultural experience and social knowledge are gained by humans through group interactions.

Fundamentally, technology is knowledge organized and applied for useful group purposes.

Logic...
Logic is where thinking and feeling challenge each other the most. Logic demands structured thinking. Feelings and emotions naturally resist such structure.

Language enables philosophy.

Language structures sounds to communicate understanding between two or more people. A common understanding based on complex mental associations; abstract yet useful metaphors.

Fundamentally, all language is metaphor.

Written language was a monumental innovation by human beings for providing the crucial capability to systematically record and exchange knowledge between large groups of different people over distances and time. The printing press and the global computer network were key technological means to leverage the accessibility, reliability and timeliness of information and knowledge.

Philosophy is based on logical, rational argument.

Rational argument based on structured thinking and reasoning. A structure of spoken or written words founded on a connected flow of supporting factors.

This is what makes up good reasoning. Bad reasoning comes from disconnected flows and unsupportable factors.

Good reasoning demonstrates connected cause and effect. Bad reasoning demonstrates confusion.

Ethics...
Values are the junction of human feeling and thinking. Our feelings for ourselves and others are tempered by our thinking of how to interact with others.

Values establish the boundary between concern for self and concern for others.

Values are principles people use for guidance on how to live their lives and how to treat other people. Ethics are the actions of applying these values.

Values define the tension between individual well-being and the well-being of others. Values establish what is right and what is wrong. Ethics (virtues) reflect rightful actions and wrongful actions.

The value of living gets down to the meaning of our human lives. Sam Harris asserts living well begins with self-respect and continues with exchanging mutual respect with others.

Self-respect and dignity are indispensable conditions of living well. When a person feels wronged, he (she) feels disrespected and experiences a loss of dignity.

The philosopher Immanuel Kant proposed we cannot respect our own humanity unless we respect humanity in others.

Aesthetics...
Feelings point the right direction.

Whereas epistemology and logic search for knowledge to find truth, aesthetics searches for beauty to find truth.

Aesthetics involves both the individual and group interpretation of beauty. This interpretation begins with an individual's perception and insight; an internal subjective experience. Feeling leads thinking.

Feelings resulting in joy, wonder, clarity, inspiration. Feelings described as beautiful.

Art provides the elegant translation of beauty to be revealed to others. Individual insight is realized and unified in others through such art. Art evokes such shared insight.

This unity of revelation and insight is the beautiful.

While the philosopher transforms thinking through the written word, the artist transforms feeling through art; both in search of understanding the human condition.

Note: Existentialism is a more recently developed philosophical approach. Individual human existence (one's feeling nature) leads essence (one's thinking nature). Individuals are viewed as independently acting, responsible, conscious beings; creating their own values and resulting meaning of life. The key value is freedom and the primary ethic is authenticity. Though there is no common definition of existentialism (which fits well with aesthetics), the ethical emphasis on individual authenticity definitely gives it an aesthetic flavor.

Politics...

Humans are evolved social beings who organize themselves into a variety of groups. Membership in such groups includes trade-offs of both costs and mutual benefits for all the involved people.

Fundamentally, people exchange individual decision-making for larger group security.

This exchange is balanced by rights and responsibilities between the group and each of the individual members. Whether implied (feeling) or defined (thinking), these exchanges result in expectations for all concerned.

Such expectations result in a method of governing the group. This includes the designation of the individual(s) with the power and authority to make the implied and defined governance decisions for the group.

Politics is the method of establishing such decision-making power.

Politics is possibly the most complex branch of philosophy. It is where the relationship between feeling ard thinking is the most dynamic; the most shifting.

If a situation or resulting decision seems crazy, it's probably political in nature.

Politics is the philosophical branch which directly affects all the people subject to the governing actions.

So What Now...
Philosophy may not be a familiar subject, but it doesn't have to be a confusing one for you.

When someone asks about your philosophy on a certain subject, you now have the opportunity to respond in fashion.

Your epistemological insight should provide the logical foundation to advance your metaphysical position fully supported by fitting ethical, aesthetic and political considerations.

Also you probably won't get asked such a question again.

Remember, the meaning of a word is its use in the language.

So embrace your springing philosophy.

For in the end, its amazing things work out as well as they do.

Party Colors

"Rule of Thumb": If a situation or resulting decision seems crazy, it's probably political in nature.

Ever wonder why the Democratic Party is represented by the color blue while the Republican Party is given the color red?

By convention on the political continuum, Liberals are placed on the left while the Conservatives are positioned on the right. Across the world liberalism has been associated with revolutionary ideals and actions. Conversely, conservativism with stability and tradition. Liberals as proponents of the people. Conservatives as respectful of the established order. The passion of the people versus the rational perspective of the powerful. The fire of the activists countered by the cooler reaction of the orthodox. The red of people's passion challenging the blue of reasoned order.

In politics a red flag has been a symbol of left-wing politics or socialism. Look at the flags of China and the former Soviet Union, both communist countries, both predominately red in color. Communists have long been known as "Reds". A "Red Flag" is a metaphor for something signaling a problem.

Wait a minute…in the United States isn't the Democratic Party associated with liberalism and the left while correspondingly the Republican Party with conservatism and the right?

22

How did the Democrats get represented by calming, soothing blue while the Republicans end up with impassionate, fiery red?

Reference Terms

Oxymoron – a contradiction of terms; a combination of two contradictory words; it may produce a dramatic effect but it does not make sense (examples: open secret, foolish wisdom, virtually true).

Paradox – a situation made up of two opposite, seemingly impossible (crazy) things but which is actually true.

The U.S. flag is red, white and blue. The color white is associated with surrender; as well as with purity. Neither party desires to be associated with defeat; nor can either party claim to be pure. Also neither party would want to be known as the "White Party" for a multitude of politically incorrect racist assumptions and allegations. (It's a wonder the term "White House" hasn't come under attack or been changed; but that's another subject).

An unnamed source attributes this political blue and red color-coding to well-known television newscaster Tom Brokaw. Knowing that liberalism was associated with the color red and conservatism with blue, he felt assigning red to Democrats would cause, nay arouse, excessive negative popular emotional reaction because of the color red's association with leftist socialism, communism, and disruptive revolution. Rather, use the color blue as a calming influence to subtly reinforce a positive perception of Democrats by the general population. By implication, who really cares about any negative association of the

23

color red with Republicans; they continually maintain their defense of red-blooded Americans.

Thus we have the media-generated convention of "Blue Democratic States" and "Red Republican States".

However, another explanation may provide the underlying (or maybe rising) reason.

Reference the results of the 2016 House of Representatives voting. The Presidential Electoral College results are by overall state results where the winner takes the whole state. This presidential method blurs the actual distribution of voting results within a state. The 435 House of Representative members are elected every two years by smaller geographic (some would say gerrymandered) districts which more accurately reflect the variation of voting results.

The resulting red-blue map presents an interesting picture of a seemingly "Red Sea" of 240 large geographical Republican districts with 195 small islands of blue Democratic districts corresponding to heavily populated areas. With the exception of Nevada, parts of Arizona, northern New Mexico, and land locked Vermont (home of Bernie Sanders), these islands of Democratic districts are located on the East Coast, the West Coast or along major rivers. Minnesota, the land of 10,000 lakes, is also predominantly blue and historically politically corrupt blue Chicago is on Lake Michigan.

Bottom line the blue Democratic-dominated districts are concentrated around blue water. These blue water areas are the most susceptible to rising waters associated with contended global warming. These Democratic districts are most at risk to be inundated by the waters of changing climatic conditions.

While one may argue that having Democrats represented by the color blue is an oxymoron (a contradiction in terms resulting in a falsehood), such color representation may actually be a paradox (apparently crazy opposite terms that reveal a hidden truth).

Maybe such Democrats are instinctively seeking to return to their evolutionary roots in the oceans.

Big Brother Approaching

Ignorance is Strength… "1984" by George Orwell

The written word was arguably the keystone innovation of human culture. The ability to capture, record and transfer ideas to others over space and time was instrumental to discovering and expanding knowledge.

Actually writing enabled the recording of many types of information. The knowledge quality of such information was dependent upon the observation, experience, repetition and acceptability by others.

It was soon discovered such written information was subject to the same individual variation and subjective bias as verbal communication between humans.

As real time dialogue offers the opportunity for others to listen before responding, the written word provides a longer delay to more fully consider the content of the communication exchange process. An opportunity for reflective response versus emotional reaction.

Though, many readers will still choose the path of least resistance provided solely by emotional reaction.

Knowledge relies on reflection. Ignorance relies on reaction. Knowledge is questioned during the short term and confirmed over the long term. Ignorance is accepted during the short term and abandoned over the long term.

Knowledge depends on learning. Ignorance thrives on notion.

Knowledge achieves respect. Ignorance desires popularity.

Knowledge requires extended attention. Ignorance survives on vague awareness.

Humans are evolved social beings. Our ability to survive and thrive is dependent upon establishing and maintaining a variety of relationships with multiple groups of people.

We possess an ongoing need to interact with others in order to ensure our individual well being. All of us desire to be recognized and appreciated by others. We will employ much energy and a variety of methods to communicate with others who share the same desires.

After the invention of writing, two key technological innovations greatly leveraged human ability to communicate over larger distances and shorter times with greater numbers of other people. These innovations were the printing press and the computer-driven global internet. The telephone, radio, television and associated electronic recording and transmission capabilities were all complimentary steps in the relentless progress and expansion of ubiquitous communication.

The exchange and analysis of data and information has increased in both importance and value. Covert espionage between countries and within countries has evolved into common business, political, governmental and military practices.

Individuals have developed parallel concerns, even paranoia, about how their personal information is being accessed and used by these same business, political, and governmental entities.

27

The human contradiction, even irony, of this invasive information accumulation is that many of the same people concerned about potential conspiracies will freely share their personal lives through the ever expanding social network exchanges. Rather than preventing "Big Brother" from forcing itself into their lives, they are willingly sharing their personal information through multiple pathways.

There is a possibility people's awareness of potential governmental intrusion would limit or restrain their willful distribution of personal information. However given human nature, such voluntary restraint seems an unlikely long term proposition. Most people can't resist the temptation to share the myriad details of their personal lives. This is continually reinforced by others who also seem to have an insatiable appetite to access, review and further exchange such information. There seems to be a bigger fear of being left out than being controlled or manipulated.

While direct communication with other individuals has dramatically increased, individual respect, consideration and courtesy appears to have correspondingly declined.

For some reason the impersonal context of electronic interaction does not provide the same social and cultural inhibitions as direct, face-to-face communication. The path of least resistance to such inhibitions continually presents itself when the immediate reaction from the other person is buffered by the very physical remoteness provided by the social media tool.

Many social media users feel little need to restrain or constrain themselves from addressing others in rude, insulting or even slanderous manners. Mutual respect is sacrificed for individual conceit.

A corresponding discourse on the parallel decline of correct spelling and proper grammar does not have to be further explained or elaborated. Suffice to say such elaboration would fall on deaf ears and disinterested offenders.

"Newspeak" (from Orwell's "1984") needs no forced imposition from an oppressive, intrusive government. What is not evolution or improvement becomes deterioration and decay. The political correctness movement demonstrates the impact of determined, prolonged and reinforced language manipulation. Fewer contrived, suitable words are deemed better than more commonly used but alleged hurtful words.

Challenge and respectful disagreement are key elements of establishing knowledge and associated truth. Freedom of speech is necessary to ensure all points of view have the opportunity to be considered. Opposing points of view must be fully expressed and compared. When such opposition is hindered or prevented, oppression replaces free speech.

While it is reasonable to expect dialogue or debate to be conducted in a courteous and respectful manner, over emphasis of non-offensive language (the root of political correctness) causes discussion to be lessened in both context and importance. Unpopular viewpoints are declared unacceptable or wrong merely because a hurtful intent is implied or perceived. Immediate feeling is more important than reflective thought.

News is reported through bits of emotion with little need for balancing context.

Rather than run the risk a reasonable person could not adequately judge rightful or wrongful intent, an unpopular view is presumed to be wrong. Thought crimes (and associated thought criminals) can not be tolerated. Hate crimes add another hurtful dimension beyond established, appropriate criminal or civil penalties.

It is argued history is written by the victors. However such history can also be modified by later prescribed viewpoints or veiled agendas.

Global warming is an interesting case in point. There is much open debate about whether the increasing use of fossil fuels has caused overall temperatures of the earth to increase over a relatively short geological time period. Geological evidence demonstrates the earth has gone through multiple cycles of warming and cooling periods.

The key recent difference is human population has grown from one billion to more than seven billion individuals over the last 200 years. Remembering it took the human race over 200,000 years to reach one billion.

A parallel knowledge-based technological increase in food production capabilities and improved medical practices has supported this dramatic population explosion.

Yet popular responses to deal with the resulting climatic and environmental effects have focused on symptoms rather than root causes. No amount of symptomatic air, water or other environmental restrictions will ever over ride the root cause of continued, unchecked population growth. Until the world's peoples, cultures and associated governments face into this root cause, overall global climatic and economic conditions will continue to worsen.

Most of the world's religious and cultural practices are based on living conditions existing some two thousand years ago. Back then birth survival rates were dramatically lower, and subsequent life spans were significantly shorter, than our current realities. Those bygone circumstances encouraged all surviving people to reproduce as much as possible.

Whereas such past procreation activities were practical survival strategies, in today's world such obsolete beliefs are ticking time bombs of eventual societal chaos. Free will requires knowledge-based decision-making to meet the dynamic challenges of all humanity.

It is ironic that Italy, the home of the Vatican, is currently a desired destination of multitudes of people from Africa trying to escape the deteriorating effects of overpopulation and its resulting poverty and lack of opportunity. Ironic because of the Vatican's avowed resistance to responsible birth control.

Sadly, though, such stated ironic viewpoints are typically denounced for disrespecting the diverse cultures of mankind. Yet all of mankind will eventually be impacted by these various forms of denial.

When God reportedly said "Let there be light", strong consideration should be given to light as a metaphor for knowledge.

Provided a future Ministry of Truth will permit such an expansive meaning of the word. Hopefully this meaning of light as knowledge will be deemed double-plus good doublespeak (ref. "Newspeak").

The Contest
(With respect and apologies to George Orwell)

Defiance is risky in certain corporate cultures.

The first time Kent Jones saw Delia was at a sidewalk café. She was sitting at the table adjacent to Kent and his two lunch companions.

Delia was eating alone while reading a book. She had looked in his direction when his group sat down at the table; the typical reactive glance when one hears new noise. She quickly returned her attention to her book.

As Kent sat down he shot a quick look in Delia's direction. The customary appraisal young males perform whenever they notice a young solitary female. His first impression was more of interest than attraction; more of curiosity. Why was she eating alone? What was she reading? Does she come here often?

However his attention was quickly diverted back to his two associates; focused on the lunch menu. After ordering, their conversation quickly shifted to recent experiences from the morning's workplace; different speculations concerning management's suspected plots to further manipulate the workforce.

Kent's friend, Tim Carsons reported, "I heard from Fullfirth in Accounting the company was going to lay-off a third of the workforce." Kent immediately heard Delia suppress a laugh.

Kent looked up in Delia's direction and said, "I'm sorry if our conversation is disturbing you."

Delia also looked up with her hand trying to cover her smirk, "You're not disturbing me. I'm afraid I was eavesdropping on your conversation. I'm sorry."

Kent quickly smiled, "No need to apologize. I can see where our conversation might be amusing to an outsider. However, we have real concerns."

Now in control, Delia replied, "I'm sure you do. But our company has the same rumors about every six months. But as they say, you're not paranoid if they're really out to get you."

Kent looked at her directly, "I'm impressed with one who is so calm in difficult situations."

Delia didn't blink, "Not calm, just experienced. Excuse me but I must be going. Don't want my boss to think I take extended lunch breaks. Good Luck with your lay-offs."

Kent called after her, "If you come back here for lunch next week, I'll give you a status update."

Delia turned slightly, "I like to eat outside when the weather is pleasant."

Tim Carsons said in a hushed voice, "Kent do you think anybody else heard us talking?"

Kent chuckled, "Don't be paranoid Carsons."

§

A week later, Kent saw Delia again having lunch by herself at the same sidewalk table. This time he was by himself. This was the second day of nice weather he had strolled by these tables.

Delia, saw him approaching out of the corner of her eye. Before, he could say anything she looked up, "Either you're on your lunch hour or wandering aimlessly in your unemployment."

Kent grinned, "Still employed. May I join you?"

Delia motioned to the open chair beside her, "Please join me. I'm Delia."

Kent carefully sat down, trying not to be too eager, "Thanks Delia. I'm Kent. Is that the same book?"

Delia responded, "No Kent, I'm a fast reader. Did your two friends get fired or were they cramping your style?"

Kent kept grinning, "Both still employed. Sometimes I have lunch alone."

After some small talk Delia's tone changed, "Kent, what company do you work for?"

Kent shrugged, "No big secret, MaxRite."

Delia nodded, "I thought so. I remember one of your friends was wearing a MaxRite jacket. What work do you do?"

Kent pursed his lips, "I work in the Information Technology department. Why?"

Delia continued, "I work for AmCap in mergers and acquisitions. Our CEO Silverberg is very interested in MaxRite."

Kent inhaled quickly, "You mean Manny Silverberg; 'the Silver Shark'!"

Delia replied, "You seem to be familiar with his reputation."

Kent could only shake his head, "He wrote the book on corporate takeovers."

Delia slyly said, "He may be perceived as cold-blooded but he's good at it."

Kent looked directly at Delia, "I'm curious, why tell me this?"

Delia slowly smiled, "I've been involved in three other AmCap acquisitions. Each time I was able to partner with someone who worked for the target company. Let's just say everyone involved profited nicely from the resulting takeovers."

Kent continued to stare at Delia, "I think that's called corporate theft; 'white collar' crime. People go to jail for that…or worse."

Delia's smile remained, "Only if one gets caught."

Kent was silent for a while, "Tell me more."

§

Corporate takeovers are a contest of wills. The more information the acquiring company knows about the target company's business, the better. While many laws are in place to regulate access to such information, other paths can be pursued.

Sid Caruthers founded MaxRite in **1984**. He detested everything Manny Silverberg and AmCap represented in business. Sid Caruthers would not hire anyone who had worked for AmCap. Anyone who voluntarily left MaxRite had to sign a "no compete" agreement stating they would not work for AmCap.

MaxRite's corporate security chief was simply known as O'Bannon. It was alleged O'Bannon had worked for the CIA and/or the mafia. There were rumors of former employees who went to work for AmCap and were never heard from again. No current or former MaxRite employee wanted to meet O'Bannon.

§

Delia told Kent she needed someone who worked in either accounting or information systems; such people had access to confidential company information.

It wasn't just coincidence Kent had first seen her at this sidewalk cafe. She had been visiting the popular area eating and drinking spots for a month. A few well placed "tips" to bartenders and waitresses had identified Kent as a potential accomplice. A private investigation firm provided additional background information on Kent. Though there was a risk a chosen person would refuse Delia's offer and report it, such methods had proven successful.

Kent Jones was a willing participant. He decided now was the time to take action; to move forward.

Given the choice of meekly waiting to see what happened or taking action for his benefit, Kent jumped at the opportunity. If the acquisition was going to happen, he wanted to be one of the survivors. All the better if he profited financially from it. Guys like Carsons and Fullfirth were the lambs being led to the slaughter.

Delia gave Kent a list of desired financial, customer and technical product information. Although he would have to be careful, Kent was confident he could obtain the identified information without being caught. He would take his time with it. Kent and Delia scheduled a dinner meeting in three weeks to exchange the pilfered information.

§

The meeting was set for 9:00 pm. Kent arrived first and procured a quiet table. Delia joined him. During dinner she quickly reviewed the flash drive of information. Satisfied, she gave Kent the account number of the foreign bank account. They left separately…

§

Two days later Kent and Tim Carsons were having lunch at the same sidewalk café. Suddenly a man walked up and quietly sat down beside Kent. There were two other very large men standing behind the uninvited guest.

The stranger gave Kent a newspaper opened up to an article. The headline read "AmCap Employee Dies in Single Auto Accident." There was a picture of Delia accompanying the article.

The stranger looked intently at Kent, "Good afternoon Mr. Jones, my name is O'Bannon."

Without shifting his stare from Kent, O'Bannon coldly said to Carsons, "You had lunch by yourself today."

One of the large men motioned in Tim's direction. Tim quickly left the table without looking back…

§

… Two days later at work, Tim Carsons saw Fullfirth from Accounting.

Fullfirth frowned, "Sorry to hear about Kent's death. That curve on Highway 101 outside of town has always been dangerous."

Tim cautiously looked around, "Shows it's always better to **GO** slow."

This short story is dedicated to my nephew Eric Blair who works for the NSA. I'm speculating another Eric Blair (pen name George Orwell) might have seen irony in an unrelated namesake working for an information-based, governmental security agency (ref. Ministry of Truth).

Ludicrous Speed

While politics craves possibilities, economics reflects practicalities.

In poker, when a player borrows money during the play of a hand, it is called "going light". If this player loses the hand, he gives his IOU, called a "marker", to the winner. Said "marker" is a debt owed to the holder of the "marker".

The speed-of-light is close to 186,000 miles per second which multiplies to traveling almost 6 trillion miles per year; better known as the astronomical distance term "light year".

The U.S. government has its own version of a "light year". The federal debt is exceeding $1 trillion a year. The U.S. is "going light" at a current rate (speed) of over $31,000 per second. The problem is this type of "going light year" is approaching the scientific astronomical term in both speed and magnitude. The total current U.S. debt has reached (traveled a distance of) over $16 trillion (this essay was written in 2013; the debt is now over $19 trillion).

That's over $54 thousand for every man, woman and child in the United States; over $154 thousand for each taxpayer; almost $300 thousand for each person who actually pays federal taxes.

The United States began as a constitutional federal republic in 1789 with George Washington as its first President. After the Declaration of Independence in 1776, the first United States government was organized under the Articles of Confederation to fight the Revolutionary War. The biggest problem with this type of government was, in the words of George Washington, "no money". It did not have the central authority (or the ability) to collect taxes and issue debt to finance its governmental operations.

Because the U.S. lacked a strong centralized financial foundation, it could not effectively govern the new country, pay its war debts, nor defend its sovereignty from foreign countries. Something had to change for the new country to survive.

Enter the U.S. Constitution and Article 1 Section 8. The Congress shall have power to:

• lay and collect taxes, duties, imposts and excises

• pay the debts and provide for the common defense and general welfare of the United States

• borrow money on the credit of the United States...

It took the country 193 years to reach $1 trillion in debt in 1982; 4 more years to reach $2 trillion in 1986; 4 more years to reach $3 trillion in 1990; 2 more years to reach $4 trillion in 1992; 4 more years to reach $5 trillion in 1996; and a whole 6 more years to reach $6 trillion in 2002.

As the astronomical distance of a light year is 6 trillion miles, one could say the U.S. debt ("going light") reached astronomical proportions at $6 trillion in 2002.

The next 11 years saw the debt continue to increase to over $16 trillion. The nearest star to Earth (other than the Sun) is Proxima Centauri 4.2 light years or 25.4 trillion miles away. At the current annual rate of debt growth, it will take about 9 more years (2022) for the debt to reach $25.4 trillion. At that point our debt will not only be astronomical but also interstellar in scale.

"Spaceballs" is a 1987 American science fiction comedy and parody film co-written and directed by Mel Brooks. "Spaceball One" was the main spacecraft of the evil galactic bad guys. With respects to "Star Wars" and "Star Trek" fans, "Spaceball One" was capable of traveling faster than the speed-of-light. It could accelerate to "light speed"; then faster to "ridiculous speed"; and finally to "ludicrous speed".

Einstein coined the term space-time to represent the "fabric" of space and time. The Star Trek series used the term "warp drive" to travel faster-than-light speed (by warping the space-time fabric). Mel Brooks' somewhat warped sense of humor took it the next step by using "ludicrous speed". "Ludicrous Speed" resulted in the ship leaving a trail of plaid (parodying the "warp trail" seen in the "Star Trek" films).

Check it out the growing national debt at www.usdebtclock.org . Look at the "U.S. National Debt" meter (kind of a dollar mileage meter). It takes some 30 seconds for the 7th number to the left (counting millions of dollars) to increase by one. While you watch, it takes a little over 30 seconds for the U.S. Debt to increase by another $1 million.

If one looks at the all the numbers on this web page together, it looks like a dynamic fabric of moving numbers; the spinning numbers appear to weave a complex plaid fabric of debt.

Our national debt has reached "Ludicrous Speed".

Most people don't know how many zeroes are in a trillion (it's twelve; count them – 1,000,000,000,000). It's even harder to get a handle on how big a trillion really is.

A trillion is a thousand-billion; a million-million. It would take a person, speaking at two words per second, nearly 16 thousand years to count to a trillion. 16 thousand years ago our ancestors were still living in caves.

One trillion one-dollar bills laid end-to-end would cover the 93 million miles distance from the Sun to the Earth; with enough left over to go to the moon and back; and then circle the earth 25 times.

A trillion seconds ago would be almost 32 thousand years ago. 32 thousand years ago our ancestors were driving the Neanderthals out of the caves.

Einstein's famous equation $E=mc^2$ also sets the maximum physical speed limit at the speed-of- light. It would take an infinite amount of energy (E) for an object to travel at the speed-of-light (c); unfortunately that much energy would cause the object to gain an infinite amount of mass (m). Bottom line the faster something speeds up, the heavier it gets, and the more difficult it is to keep it moving.

Just like the speed-of-light and the mass of an object, the faster we spend our borrowed debt dollars, the heavier the debt becomes; and the harder it is to keep our economy moving.

Just like the physical speed limit of light, there is a fiscal speed limit of debt spending. Just like there is no infinite amount of energy or mass, there is no infinite amount of debt.

The fiscal fabric of economic supply and demand is woven together by the threads of a sound monetary system. Such threads become weaker and weaker when stretched by heavier and heavier debt. It is only a matter of time before our economy starts unraveling.

Our present and future economy is becoming more and more warped by the ludicrous speed of our national debt spending.

Unfortunately, the joke's on us.

Human nature may be idealistic in hope; but it's realistic in application.

Human Nature Fact #1: Circumstances which are allowed to persist over time become "normal" in people's minds, regardless of the original intent. Sooner or later problems occur when people come to believe they are entitled to such easy circumstances.

The difference between possibility and probability is practicality.

Maybe we should let the gambling bookmakers (better known as "bookies") take over the practical management of the national debt from Congress. Bookies have a well-known reputation for minimizing debt accumulation and reliably maximizing debt collection.

Congressional bettors might think twice about "going light" because they know they would be held both fiscally responsible and physically accountable for their "markers".

However considering we're talking about people and politicians, maybe all of this is so impractical that it has to be ludicrous.

Oppoortunities

The fantasy of the American Dream

Forget such mundane activities as practical education, hard work, ethical business practices or responsible government.

For most Americans in today's globally-connected world, the best chances for personal freedom and financial security lie in one of the following options.

Best Options:
A) Win the lotto (except in Illinois because you might not get paid).
B) Get a large insurance settlement and/or win a civil lawsuit (The U.S. has about 5% of the world's population and some 50% of the world's lawyers).
C) Be declared "disabled" and receive ongoing cash payments from the government (the Feds can always get more money from someplace).
D) Secure a full-time pay/benefit government job (really helps if you are connected politically).

Celebrity Options:
E) Become a professional athlete in the NFL, NBA, MLB, NHL, PGA or a NASCAR driver (though most people do not possess the requisite ability and have a better chance with the first four options).
F) Become a major celebrity actor, singer, artist, model, television show host or national newscaster (though these also require some nebulous perceived talent and therefore

most people still have a more realistic shot with the first four options).

Default Option:
G) Continue to feel entitled to experience a good life just because you're a part of the 5% of the world's exploding population who live in the United States (but don't worry the freely spending, continually growing Federal governmental agencies will take care of you by borrowing more money than can ever be repaid).

Unexciting Knowledge is Power Option:
H) Learn mathematics and associated practical work skills to compete for the increasingly complex technology-based occupations (ignoring the fact the studious Chinese have more honors students than the U.S. has students; also don't forget the equally numerous scholarly Indians).

Some realistic odds:
Illinois Lotto: 1 winning chance in 20,358,520 (about 1 person in either Florida or New York)
Powerball: 1 winning chance in 292,201,338 (about 1 person in the United States)

When individual pursuits for personal well-being are better met by chance success than by personal effort, it is called faint hope.

The U.S. continues to add about $100 billion a month to its current national debt of over $18 trillion (that's trillion with twelve zeroes). A legacy of debt obligation to be inherited by our descendants (better known as children, grandchildren, great grandchildren...).

45

When a country's pursuits for its citizens' well-being are based on oblivious and foolhardy spending efforts, it is called despair.

It's more than economic, social or political failure, it's a failure of practical action. If this continues, most American children will not enjoy the American Dream but suffer a post-American Nightmare.

On Jan. 4, 2016 the Powerball lottery had rolled over to $400 million (it would take a person earning a $100,000 a year a mere 4000 years to earn $400 million). All the U.S. needs is 250 such Powerball winners in January 2016 (8 winners a day) to donate their winnings to cover the month's $100 billion shortfall of federal spending (if Warren Buffet donated his total fortune of $60 billion, he could cover about 2 ½ weeks of federal overspending).

Then it would only take another such 2750 generous Powerball winners over the rest of 2016 to prevent the U.S. Government from accumulating another $1.1 trillion dollars in debt.

After that it would only take another 45,000 such Powerball winners to pay-off the remaining $18 trillion of federal debt (don't worry about who's going to come up with the Powerball lottery money, just tell people it's going for a good cause).

On the other hand, if every one of the 7.5 billion people on the Earth buys around $2400 in Powerball tickets this year and donates the proceeds to the U.S., we could eliminate the federal debt (don't worry that the average world person's annual income is around $2900; it would still leave this average person $500 for food, shelter, clothing, medical care, etc. for the rest of the year).

And to be clear this doesn't buy the U.S. anything, it just pays off this existing huge IOU for money already spent for somewhat questionable returns.

And don't worry about current or future needs of the country. If the national debt gets paid off, then there should be a high level of confidence by U.S. voters that future elected representatives and leaders will not allow us to get into another similar situation by spending more than is gathered in taxes. Keeping in mind the 50% of Americans who actually pay federal taxes (though it's probably their fault for not paying more taxes to begin with; don't they know a lot of other people depend on them).

It's either that or the U.S. Congress should replace the "Star Spangled Banner" national anthem by Francis Scott Key with "Don't Worry, Be Happy" by Bobby McFerrin or "Happy" by Pharrel Williams. Of course making sure Mr. McFerrin or Mr. Williams gets paid a royalty every time the new national anthem is played.

When the future practical survival of our country is becoming a cruel joke, at least we should be entertained.

The Speed of Darkness

Attention Span Data (Reference Statistic Brain Research Institute):
- The average attention span in 2000: 12 seconds
- The average attention span in 2015: 8.2 seconds
- The average attention span of a **goldfish**: 9 seconds
- Average number of times per hour an office worker checks their e-mail inbox: 30
- Average length watched of an internet video: 2.7 minutes
- Per cent of words read on web pages of **111** words or less: 49%
- Per cent of words read on an average web page of 593 words: 28%
- Users spend only 4.4 seconds more for each additional 100 words

(Note: **110** words to this point)

Where light ends, darkness begins.

Aldous Huxley died on November 22, 1963. On any other day of that year, his death would have drawn significant attention of both newspaper and television reporters.

However, President Kennedy's assassination on that day pushed all other potential notable events far down from the public awareness. Significantly, some might say ironically, the prime communication media of the assassination events was provided by television.

Aldous Huxley was probably best known for his 1932 dystopian novel "Brave New World". This book projected a frightening futuristic world of planned human genetics, artificial human gestation methods, manipulated childhood development, dictatorial social structure and wide spread use of a pleasure enhancing drug (*soma*) to control and direct an obedient population.

In 1958 Huxley was interviewed by Mike Wallace, the later well-known reporter for CBS's *60 Minutes*. In the course of this interview Huxley outlined his major concerns for the future:

- the difficulties and dangers of world overpopulation (then some 2.8 billion people compared to the current 7.5 billion)
- the tendency toward distinctly hierarchical social organizations (based on financial influence, political power, specialized education and restricted lifestyles)
- the crucial importance of evaluating the use of technology in mass societies susceptible to wily persuasion (leveraged by expanding technological devices)
- the tendency to promote modern politicians to a naïve, accepting public as well-marketed commodities (popularity of form over substance of content)

In the foreword of his 1985 book "*Amusing Ourselves to Death*", social critic Neil Postman contrasted the worlds of George Orwell's "*1984*" (published in 1949) with Huxley's "*Brave New World*" (published in 1932).

- What Orwell feared were those who would ban books. What Huxley feared was that there would be no reason to ban a book; for there would be no one who wanted to read one.
- Orwell feared those in power who would deprive us of information. Huxley feared those who would give us so much information that we would be reduced to passivity and self-interest.
- Orwell feared the truth would be concealed from us. Huxley feared the truth would be drowned in a sea of irrelevance.
- Orwell feared we would become a captive culture. Huxley feared we would become a trivial culture; preoccupied with some equivalent of the "feelies" (multi-media methods to stimulate pleasurable sensations).

In *"1984"*, Orwell projected people were controlled by inflicting pain. In *"Brave New World"*, Huxley imagined people were controlled by inflicting pleasure.

In short, Orwell feared our fears would ruin us. Huxley feared our desires would ruin us.

Postman differentiated the Orwellian vision of the future - where totalitarian governments seize individual rights - from that offered by Aldous Huxley - where people medicate themselves into bliss; thereby voluntarily sacrificing their rights.

Drawing an analogy with Huxley's scenario, Postman saw television's entertainment value as a present-day *soma (pleasure drug)* by which citizens' rights are exchanged for consumers' entertainment.

The essential premise of Postman's book is "the form excludes the content". That is, a particular communication medium can only support a particular level of ideas. Thus rational argument, an essential of print communication, is significantly diminished through the medium (form) of television.

Because of this diminished capability, television dilutes complex subjects such as politics, religion and education. Accordingly the "news of the day" becomes a packaged commodity. Television de-emphasizes the quality of information in favor of satisfying the far-reaching needs of entertainment. Such entertainment overwhelms any relevant information.

Postman asserted the presentation of television news (satirically portrayed in 1976's *"Network"* and 1987's *"Broadcast News"* motion pictures) is a form of entertainment programming. Postman argued inclusion of theme music, the interruption of commercials, and "talking hairdos" bear witness that televised news cannot readily be taken seriously. As television is programmed according to ratings, its content is determined by commercial feasibility. Thus television fails to satisfy the conditions for honest intellectual involvement and rational argument.

In *"Brave New World Revisited"* (published in 1958) Huxley stated his apprehensions about, "the development of a vast mass communications industry; concerned in the main neither with the true nor the false, but with the more or less totally irrelevant." He concluded, "Civil libertarians and rationalists, in a word, had failed to take into account man's almost infinite appetite for distractions." Huxley further determined, "A society, most of whose members spend a great part of their time not in the here and now, but some-where else - in the irrelevant other worlds of sport and soap opera, of mythology and metaphysical fantasy - will find it hard to resist the encroachments of those who would manipulate and control the present."

Reading exacts intense intellectual involvement. Only in the printed word can complex truths be rationally conveyed. Postman gives a striking example. Many of the first fifteen U.S Presidents (those before Lincoln) could probably have walked down the street without being recognized by the average citizen. Yet all those men would have been quickly known by their written words. However, the reverse is true today. The names of Presidents or even famous preachers, lawyers, and scientists call up visual images; typically television images. But few, if any, of their words come to mind. The few that do almost exclusively consist of carefully chosen soundbites.

Thomas Jefferson held, "If a nation expects to be ignorant and free, it expects what never was and never will be." He added, "The people cannot be safe without information. Where the press is free, and every man able to read, all is safe."

However neither Jefferson nor Huxley could have foreseen today's world of ubiquitous web-based information; much of which is comprised of emotionally-based social media with minimal concern for in-depth analysis or supporting facts. This situation is further compounded by the ever decreasing levels of focused attention applied to this ever increasing flood of information.

Huxley coined the phrase "herd-poisoning" to represent the rapid mass acceptance of unproven yet popular beliefs or viewpoints (memes). His great dread was the purposeful, manipulative use of the mass communication media of television as a catalyst for spreading irrational herd-poisoning.

One can only speculate on Huxley's reaction to the pervasive web-based media and variety of social networking tools currently in use throughout the world.

Huxley feared an unexciting truth would be eclipsed by a thrilling falsehood leveraged thorough mass media. He knew a skillful massive appeal to passion is often too strong for even the best of individual, rational principles.

Huxley did offer a potential solution; maybe more of a hope. Unlike the compliant masses, thinking individuals have a taste for rationality and an interest in facts. Their critical habit of applying their attentive minds makes them resistant to the kind of propaganda that works so well on the susceptible herds; regardless of the media being utilized. Humanity's future - indeed hope - ultimately relies, as it always has, on human intelligence.

With respect (and apologies) to John Donne's *"For Whom the Bell Tolls"*.

For I am involved in mankind.
Therefore, send not to know
For whom the goldfish stares down.
It stares down thee.

"The Speed of Darkness" first appeared in the Summer-Fall 2016 Edition of "The Rockford Review" published by the Rockford Writers' Guild.

A Day in Dallas

"What If" - The eternal question from history

November 22, 1963 dawned crisp and clear in the Dallas-Fort Worth area. President Kennedy had spent the night in Fort Worth, Texas. His schedule called for him to attend a breakfast there before departing on a short flight to Dallas later on that morning. He and his wife Jackie, along with Texas Governor John Connally and his wife Nellie, would ride in the lead limousine of a motorcade parade through downtown Dallas. The motorcade would then proceed to the Dallas Trade Mart for a luncheon speech. After the speech the presidential entourage would board Air Force One for the return trip to Washington DC.

This reason for this trip was to gain political favor in Texas in preparation for the upcoming 1964 Presidential Election. Vice President Lyndon Johnson, a Texan, recommended President Kennedy make this trip. Texas was definitely a divided state in regards to Kennedy and the Democrats. Johnson, the master politician, knew the charismatic presidential couple would make a positive impact on the Texas populace. Fact be known, Jackie Kennedy was a bigger sensation than the President. A realty not lost to either Johnson or Kennedy's chief-of-staff Kenny O'Donnell. As Texas would be a key state in the upcoming election, Kennedy agreed to the trip.

§

J. D. Tippit was a 39 year old Texas native and 11 year veteran of the Dallas Police Department. He had served in the 17th Airborne Division in World War II and was decorated with the Bronze Star. During his time on the police force he was cited twice for bravery. He and his wife

Marie had been happily married for 17 years with three children. Tippit's current patrol area was in the residential area of Oak Cliff south of downtown Dallas. This morning he was also on call as back-up for the downtown area as many of the Dallas police force were assigned for crowd control along the planned presidential motorcade route through downtown Dallas. Large crowds were expected.

Jack Ruby was the proprietor of the Carousel Club nightclub located in downtown Dallas as well as the Vegas Club in the Oak Lawn district north of downtown. He was 52 years old and had been born in Chicago as Jacob Rubenstein. He had a troubled childhood with multiple juvenile delinquency and truancy episodes, spending sporadic time in foster homes. Jack was drafted into the army in World War II and served honorably as an aircraft mechanic. After the war he returned to Chicago before moving to Dallas in 1947 and changing his name to Jack Ruby. He went onto manage various nightclubs and strip clubs. In the course of his business dealings he had developed many ties to Dallas police officers who frequented his establishments. Ruby was single, never married, with no children.

Lee Harvey Oswald was, to say the least, a complex individual. Maybe confused would be a better description; definitely frustrated with his life. He was 24 years old; born in New Orleans. His father died two months before Lee was born. His mother Marquerite moved Lee and his older brother Robert multiple times between New Orleans, New York and Dallas. Lee experienced a variety of problems growing up and was placed for a short time in a juvenile reformatory in New York for truancy. He was described as being withdrawn, temperamental and confrontational. By the age of 17, Lee had lived at 22 different places and attended 12 different schools. Lee quit school at 17 and joined the Marine Corps to be trained as a radar operator. He was eventually stationed in Japan where he taught himself Russian.

After receiving a hardship discharge allegedly based on his mother's care needs, Lee embarked on a series of bizarre actions. He defected to the Soviet Union in 1959. Though the Soviet authorities were initially suspicious, Lee managed to convince them to let him live there. He eventually was assigned to work as a lathe operator in an electronics factory in Minsk. Lee eventually married his Russian wife Marina in April 1961. Apparently disillusioned with Soviet life, Lee, Marina and their baby daughter successfully applied for immigration back to the U.S. in June, 1962. They returned to the Dallas area with little public notice; much to Lee's disappointment.

After multiple job failures in Dallas, Lee returned to New Orleans in April, 1963. Marina's new found friend Ruth Paine later drove a pregnant Marina and her daughter to New Orleans to join Lee. In late September 1963, after Lee experienced more failed jobs and a baffling association with the "Fair Play for Cuba" political front organization, Ruth Paine moved Marina and the baby back to Ruth's home in Irving, Texas. Lee then took a bus trip to Mexico City in an even more puzzling attempt to obtain a visa to go to Cuba. When the visa was refused, Lee returned to Dallas in October, 1963.

One of Ruth Paine's neighbor's, Wesley Frazier, worked at the Texas School Book Depository in downtown Dallas. Frazier helped Lee get a job there as an order-filler on October 16. Lee and Marina were experiencing marital problems. So during the work week, Lee stayed at a rooming house in Oak Cliff, south of downtown Dallas. On Friday nights he would ride with Frazier out to Irving to stay with Marina at Ruth Paine's house. Then on Monday mornings he would ride back to Dallas with Frazier.

On Wednesday afternoon, Nov. 20th Roy Truly, the School Book Depository's building manager, approached Lee Oswald on the sixth floor as Lee was filling an order. "Hey Lee, how's it going? Did you know President Kennedy's motorcade is driving right by here on Elm Street this Friday?"

Lee looked up and replied, "Hi Roy. Really? Sounds like a big day for Dallas. We should be able to get a real close look as he passes by."

After exchanging a few more pleasantries, Roy left to check on other employees. He didn't see the wry smile forming on Lee's lips.

§

Jack Ruby looked around the Carousel Club. It was close to 11 pm Thursday night, Nov. 21st. He was smiling his familiar wide grin. Business was really good; better than usual. Jack thought to himself, "Must be all the people in town to see the President's parade through Dallas tomorrow. Thank you Mr. President!"

Jack gave a quick call to his other establishment, the Vegas Club up in Oak Lawn. Business there was also exceptionally good. Even though it was only Thursday, Jack decided to drive up there around closing time. He didn't like the idea of leaving the unusually high nightly cash receipts on the premises before the weekend even

58

started.   One thing he learned in Chicago was don't encourage robbery by leaving a lot of money on the premises. It was common local knowledge that Jack was armed when he was carrying money. Additionally, Jack had a good relationship with the Dallas police. It was also rumored Ruby was somehow connected to the Chicago mob.

Besides, Jack always liked going to the Vegas Club; a slightly different clientele frequented that establishment. Even in 1963 Dallas, the Vegas Club had a good reputation within the homosexual community; though the word "gay" was beginning to gain favor as an acceptable term.   Bottom line, Jack enjoyed their unconventional sense of humor. Plus, they liked to spend their money.

It was well after 2 am when Jack left to drive up to the Vegas Club, north of downtown Dallas. He had placed the Carousel Club's plentiful nightly receipts in the Carousel's office safe.   As the Carousel Club was located in the downtown area, close to the main police station, Jack felt the money was secure. Ruby told his bar manager he was going up to check on the Vegas Club. Jack instructed the bar manager to close up when the last customers left. Jack planned on coming back later to the Carousel with the Vegas Club receipts for deposit in the office safe. Depending on the time, he would either go home or sleep on the cot in the office.   Jack wanted to watch the President's downtown parade scheduled for the following noon.

Jack arrived at the Vegas Club a little after 3 am. There was still a large crowd having a good time. Even though official closing time was 2 am, Jack had an "understanding" with the police. Besides with the presidential visit, even more slack was in effect. Many of the regular customers heartily greeted Jack on his arrival. Jack's club manager nodded to Jack; it had been a very lucrative night. Ruby smiled and nodded back. It looked like it was time to have a couple of drinks with the customers.

§

Friday morning Nov. 22nd, Lee Oswald woke up before his wife Marina. Lee had unexpectedly rode back to Irving with Wesley Frazier last night (Thursday). Usually Oswald stayed at his boarding room in Oak Cliff during the week and came back to Irving on Friday night. The only explanation Lee gave Marina and Ruth Paine was he missed Marina and the children.

Lee was very quiet so he would not wake either Marina or the new baby. He quietly dressed. Before leaving, Lee took off his wedding ring and placed it in a small china cup on the top of the dresser. He also took $170 in cash from his wallet and left it beside the ring. Then Oswald went to the Paine's garage and brought out a long package covered with brown wrapping paper. He walked to the street curb where Wesley Frazier was waiting in his car for Lee.

Lee opened the back door, placed the package in the back seat and closed the door. As he got into the car on the passenger's side Lee greeted Frazier, "Morning Wesley."

Wesley replied, "Good Morning Lee. What's in the package?"

Lee casually said, "Just some curtain rods for my room in Oak Cliff. Remember I told you that was the reason I came back last night. Let's get going. You were the one who wanted to leave early for work today."

Frazier nodded, "Oh yeah, I remember. Yeah with the President's parade today there will probably be more downtown traffic. You know how backed up it can get around there."

Lee sarcastically responded, "Sure, we don't want to delay those important text books from getting delivered on time."

§

Officer J.D. Tippit was also up earlier than usual. Tippit's shift sergeant had instructed all his men to be on patrol an hour earlier. With the upcoming presidential motorcade through downtown, heavier traffic and large crowds were expected along the planned parade route. As a designated back-up, J. D. was expected to handle normal police calls to free up the assigned patrol officers to maintain visibility along the motorcade route.

Therefore Officer Tippit was on duty by 6 am. He purposely located himself along the southern portion of the downtown area, a little north of his regular Oak Cliff patrol area. Even though the President was not scheduled to arrive at Love Field until 11 am, traffic was noticeably heavier and people were starting to arrive at prime viewing points along the announced parade route. J. D. wondered if he would get lucky and see the President and Jackie drive by.

§

Jack Ruby shook his head again. He was trying to keep awake as he was driving back from the Vegas Club to the Carousel Club downtown. The late night customers at the

Vegas Club did themselves proud partying. It took all of his and the club manager's persuasive skills to get the last of the revelers out of the Vegas Club around 5 am. Then it took another half hour to close up the club and reconcile the night's cash receipts. Jack also had to retrieve his dog sleeping in the office and carry her to the car along with the briefcase of cash receipts.

Jack was driving south from Oak Lawn on Turtle Creek and Cedar Spring Road. He was going to cut over to North Field Street and then over to Houston. Once on Houston he would proceed downtown and take a left onto Commerce to get to the Carousel Club. There he would deposit these cash receipts in the office safe. Ruby decided he would sleep on the office cot and get up to see the presidential motorcade as it passed through a block away on Main Street. Just before reaching the Continental Avenue intersection something caused his dog to suddenly wake up with a yelp. This caught Jack by surprise and almost by reflex he turned his sleepy gaze towards the dog; thus failing to recognize and respond to the red light at the intersection.

§

Since leaving the Paine house in Irving, Lee Oswald maintained his silence. In the short time Wesley Frazier had known Oswald, such behavior was not surprising. Wesley just accepted Oswald's moodiness; experience had shown Lee would talk when he felt like it.

Frazier had traveled along Irving Boulevard, to North Riverside Boulevard and then onto Continental Avenue. Wesley smiled to himself. Traffic was becoming heavier as they approached the downtown area. Wesley didn't expect

Lee to compliment him on the decision to leave early. As they approached the intersection with Houston Street, the light had already turned green. Wesley slowed to make the right turn onto Houston.

Suddenly without warning, Jack Ruby's car barreled through the intersection and struck the left rear part of Frazier's car; causing it to violently spin to the left, across the lane and into the opposing traffic lane. This exposed Oswald on the passenger's side to an oncoming delivery truck.

The delivery truck had no chance to brake or steer to avoid Frazier's spinning vehicle. It struck the car directly at the passenger's door, crushing Oswald on impact.

Officer Tippit responded to the emergency call and was the first to arrive at the crash scene. He immediately called for an ambulance, and additional police support. Even with his 11 years of experience as a police officer, J.D. was taken aback. This was a bad accident.

§

Officer Tippit pulled his police car in front of Frazier's smashed car; keeping the flashing red lights of his vehicle turned-on to warn the oncoming traffic. The delivery truck had stopped askew in the middle of the road beside Frazier's car. As the passenger side door was crushed inward, Tippit knew he could not open it. Tippit approached the driver's door and slowly opened it. J.D. observed Frazier was conscious but appeared dazed.

In a clear, stern voice Tippit spoke, "Sir. Are you all right? Can you hear me?"

63

Frazier slowly turned his head towards Tippit, "I think so. What happened?"

Looking into Frazier's eyes J.D. responded, "Your car was hit by another vehicle. An ambulance is on the way."

Frazier slowly nodded his head.

Tippit then focused his attention past Frazier towards Oswald's unconscious body, "You in the passenger's seat, can you hear me?"

No response. Tippit could hear the sirens of the approaching police cars and ambulance.

Again speaking to Frazier, "Sir the ambulance is almost here. Hang on."

Tippit stood up and motioned the approaching ambulance towards Frazier's car. As the two supporting police cars arrived, J.D. motioned one towards Ruby's car now stopped on the other side of the intersection and the other towards the delivery truck.

Two ambulance attendants came up to Frazier's car. They helped Frazier out of the car. As he could walk, an attendant helped Frazier into the back of the ambulance. The other attendant crawled in across the seat, lightly grabbed Oswald's left shoulder and gently shook him, "Sir, can you hear me! Sir, can you say anything!"

No response.

By this time the other ambulance attendant had returned. The two attendants managed to retrieve Oswald's still unconscious body from the wrecked car. With Tippit's help, the three of them placed Oswald on the wheeled gurney, pushed it over to the ambulance and loaded it into the rear of the ambulance. The ambulance then sped away with flashing red lights and blasting siren, on its way to Parkland Hospital.

By this time two more police cars and another ambulance had arrived on the scene.

Tippit observed the driver of the delivery van was uninjured but understandingly shaken. The driver was standing by the van, talking to the police officer who had stopped there.

Tippit then looked across the street towards Ruby's car, noticing the front end was crumpled and the radiator steaming. Another policeman was talking to the driver, who was still in the car but apparently conscious and coherent. The second ambulance had stopped and the two attendants helped the driver out of the car and into the ambulance.

As the driver emerged from the car, Tippit recognized him as Jack Ruby. Even though Tippit had never met him, he knew Ruby by reputation. Tippit shook his head slowly. At this point two wrecker trucks arrived to retrieve the involved vehicles. Tippit turned his attention back to getting the accident scene cleared and getting traffic safely flowing again; remembering this was during the morning rush hour.

The two other recently arrived police officers had positioned themselves to direct traffic around the accident scene. One wrecker truck was preparing to remove Frazier's car; the other had stopped by Ruby's car. The policeman talking to the delivery truck driver yelled over to Tippit that a third wrecker truck had been summoned to tow away the damaged delivery truck. Tippit walked back to Frazier's car.

Tippit walked around the wrecked car, perusing its overall condition for his accident report. J.D. looked in the back seat. There on the floor was a bolt action rifle with a telescopic sight sticking out of some brown wrapping paper. Tippit told the wrecker driver not to touch anything and to tow the car to the police impound yard; not to the wrecker's repair garage.

Tippit radioed his shift sergeant and updated him on the status of the accident. Tippit informed the sergeant about the discovery of the rifle in the car. Even though this was Texas, fortress of the 2nd Amendment, something didn't feel right.

§

The ambulance containing Wesley Frazier and Lee Oswald took about 10 minutes to travel to Parkland Memorial Hospital.

Oswald was taken to the Emergency Room at Parkland Hospital. He was pronounced dead on arrival. The preliminary cause of death was recorded as blunt head trauma. As it was an accidental death, a formal autopsy would have to be performed.

Frazier was diagnosed with a possible concussion but no other severe injuries. He was shaken and somewhat dazed but conscious. Frazier was able to make a statement to an attending police officer. As he knew Oswald personally, Frazier was able to provide Oswald's next-of-kin information as well as employer information.

The attending policeman telephoned the Irving, Texas police department so Marina Oswald could be contacted about Lee's accidental death.

Frazier was able to contact his wife, who later came to the hospital to pick him up. After a short time of observation, Frazier was released with directions to follow-up with his own physician.

The second ambulance containing Jack Ruby arrived at Parkland some 15 minutes after the first ambulance. Ruby was given a thorough evaluation. Other than a slight bump on the head, he appeared to be in good health. Jack was more concerned about the status of his dog and his briefcase of cash receipts from the Vegas Club. Both the dog and the briefcase had made the trip to the hospital in the same ambulance. Ruby told the medical attendants he still wanted to get back downtown to view the President's parade. Jack was not happy when the attending police officer informed Ruby that he would, at the least, receive a citation for reckless driving.

Jack's immediate response being, "We'll see about that!"

After completing a police report at the hospital Ruby was released along with his dog and briefcase. Jack called for a taxi. There was still time to get the money into the office safe and then go observe the presidential motorcade.

§

Ron Truly, building manager for the Texas Schoolbook Depository, hung up the phone. Wesley Frazier had called him from home, informing Ron of the earlier auto accident and Lee Oswald's resulting death.

Ron shook his head. Lee had only worked there a little over a month. Ron thought Lee was a good worker; a little bit moody at times but he got the job done.

Ron was grateful Wesley was unhurt. Ron went to inform the other employees of this situation. Besides, most people were excited about the President's motorcade passing directly in front of their building that day.

Later in the day around 12:30 pm, the presidential motorcade came down Main Street and turned right onto Houston Street for one block. The presidential limousine then proceeded to take a left onto Elm Street, slowly passing the Texas Schoolbook Depository.

It was a clear, sunny day. Enthusiastic crowds had cheered the President and Jackie Kennedy throughout the entire parade route.

Local businessman Abraham Zapruder had positioned himself down the street from the Depository building; hoping to get a clear view of the passing motorcade to film with his Bell & Howell home movie camera.

As his wife steadied him, Zapruder filmed the passing presidential limousine, feeling he could almost touch the smiling JFK and his beautiful wife Jackie, in her pretty pink outfit, waving to the crowd.

After the motorcade passed, Zapruder turned to his wife and excitedly exclaimed, "Wasn't that extraordinary! I really got some great footage. I can't wait to see it."

§

The motorcade then drove onto the Dallas Trade Mart. President Kennedy gave a short luncheon speech. However, the highlight of the event was when he introduced Jackie to the large attending crowd. The thundering ovation for Jackie drowned out any subsequent applause for the President.

After the Trade Mart luncheon, the presidential limousine proceeded to Loves Field. The President's entourage boarded Air Force One for an uneventful return flight to Washington D.C.

During the flight back, Kenny O'Donnell reviewed the trip with President Kennedy. "Well Mr. President, that went very well."

JFK smiled, "Maybe we should get Jackie to run for President. If she can charm Texas, she'd be a lock to win."

Both O'Donnell and the President laughed loudly.

"A Day in Dallas: What If – The Eternal Question of History" was originally published in "Ten Short Stories by Nine Authors"; edited by Edward Grosek.

Personal Postscript

My 13th birthday occurred on November 22, 1963. I have since wondered "what if" the events of that day in Dallas had turned out differently.

Next Days in Dallas

History flows through many linkages.

Police Officer J.D. Tippit woke up earlier than usual for a Saturday morning. Especially since he was not scheduled for work.   Yesterday, Friday, November 22, 1963, had been a somewhat hectic day for the Dallas Police Department.   The whole city had been excited about President Kennedy's visit which included a motorcade parade through downtown Dallas.   The weather had cooperated with a mild, sunny day.   Large, exuberant crowds had greeted and cheered President and Mrs. Kennedy throughout the entire parade route.

Upon completion of the parade, President Kennedy made a short luncheon speech at the Dallas Trade Mart and then flew back to Washington D.C. on Air Force One. It was interesting that most of the press and TV coverage of the Presidential visit focused more on Jackie Kennedy's presence than anything President Kennedy said or did.

Unfortunately Officer Tippit didn't have a chance to see the Presidential motorcade. He was on expanded patrol duty during the parade to free up other officers for parade security. Because of this expanded duty, he responded to an early morning fatal automobile accident not far from the end of the parade route.

Something about the accident was still bothering Tippit. He couldn't really describe it. Something just felt strange.

Tippit was the first police officer to arrive at the accident scene. Apparently a car ran a stop light on Houston Street and struck the rear of another car making a right turn from Continental. The struck car was pushed into the path of an oncoming delivery truck. The delivery truck collided with the struck car at the right front door. This impact caused the death of the passenger riding in the impacted car. Fortunately the driver of this car sustained only minor injuries. The driver of the delivery truck was uninjured as well as the driver of the car which had apparently ran the red light.

As the accident scene was being cleared, Officer Tippit noticed something in the back seat floor of the struck vehicle. The something was a rifle with a telescopic sight partially covered with brown wrapping paper. Reacting more on a hunch, Tippit instructed the driver of the responding wrecker truck to tow this car to the police impound lot. After the accident scene was cleared, Tippit radioed his patrol sergeant a summary report. Tippit requested a detective inspect the accident vehicle and the curious wrapped rifle.

Something else was on Tippit's mind. Though he had never met Jack Ruby, Tippit recognized him as the driver of the other car. Jack was well known to Dallas police officers and a frequent visitor to area police stations. As Ruby was the owner and operator of two well-known "night" clubs, Tippit was surprised to see him up and about so early in the morning. Tippit guessed Ruby had probably not been to bed yet.

Tippit was also interested about the personal details of the driver and deceased passenger of the impacted car. He wanted to review the police report obtained at the receiving hospital; guessing the accident victims were taken to Parkland Hospital.

Even though he was off duty this Saturday, Tippit called the main police station to check on the status of the accident information. The Duty Sergeant told Tippit the accident report had been filed from the intake officer at Parkland Hospital. A detective had retrieved the rifle from the towed vehicle and secured it in the evidence room. Potential charges involving Ruby were still pending due to the death of the passenger. As it was the weekend, Tippit would not be able to review the various reports or talk to the detective before Monday. Tippit resigned himself to the fact he would just have to wait to get more information. Maybe the extra time would calm Tippit's uneasiness.

§

Detective Jim Leavelle was assigned the task of checking out the accident vehicle identified by Officer Tippit. After identifying the car in the police impound yard, Leavelle checked the glove box and discovered the car was registered to Wesley Frazier. Frazier was also identified as the driver of the vehicle in the accident report. Detective Leavelle had no trouble finding the partially wrapped rifle lying on the back seat floor.

Following procedures, the detective wore gloves as he carefully removed the brown paper wrapping material. A telescopic sight was mounted on the bolt-action rifle.

Leavelle did not immediately recognize the type of rifle; but he knew it was not an American model. The weapon was later identified as an Italian Model 1 Carcano rifle. The rifle's box magazine contained 5 rounds of 6.5 mm ammunition with a spent round in the chamber. Leavelle noted experienced shooters often placed an empty shell casing in the chamber to help keep the mechanism clean before firing. Leavelle's first impression was this kind of rifle was not used for hunting; least ways not in Texas. Further investigation of the vehicle's interior and trunk revealed nothing out of the ordinary. The detective secured the rifle in the police evidence room and completed the required documentation.

§

The following Monday Officer Tippit was back to work at his normal Oak Cliff patrol area. As it was a slow day, Tippit used his lunch break to go to central police headquarters to review the completed accident reports from Parkland Hospital as well as Detective Leavelle's report on the discovered rifle. Officer Tippit learned the accident car's driver, Wesley Frazier, and the deceased passenger, Lee Oswald, both worked at the Texas Book Depository Building. Frazier had reported they were on their way to work last Friday morning when struck by the other (Ruby's) car. Frazier also added Oswald normally wouldn't have been riding with him on a Friday morning. Frazier stated it was a shame Lee chose that day to bring back some curtain rods for his rented room in Oak Cliff; otherwise Lee wouldn't have been in the car that morning.

Tippit's first impression was the rifle must have belonged to Oswald. But why did Frazier think the package contained curtain rods? It was also an interesting coincidence Oswald's rooming house was in Tippit's normal patrol area.

Tippit decided to drive by the scene of the accident again. At the intersection of Continental and Houston he parked the patrol car and then walked around. It was an open area with good visibility. According to the report taken at the hospital, Ruby reported he was distracted by his dog and didn't see the red light. Considering the time of day, Tippit thought it was just as likely Ruby fell asleep at the wheel. With a resulting fatality, Ruby was at risk for a vehicular homicide charge; at the least a reckless driving citation.

As Tippit drove back downtown on Houston Street he noticed the turn onto Elm Street went right by the Texas School Book Depository Building; the place of employment for both Frazier and Oswald. It suddenly dawned on him this was the route of the Presidential motorcade. Officer Tippit again parked his patrol car and entered the Depository Building. At the front desk he identified himself and asked to see the manager. In a short time, Ron Truly appeared and escorted Tippit to his office.

Officer Tippit explained he was the lead police officer at the scene of the automobile accident and was consequently doing some follow-up. Truly nodded his understanding and offered his assistance. Truly openly responded to Tippet's questions about Frazier's and Oswald's respective work records. Wesley Frazier was a well-regarded, relatively long term employee. Lee Oswald had only worked there for about a month but had demonstrated reliability and good attendance. Tippet asked to see where each man worked.

Tippit actually met Frasier who had returned to work that very day. Tippit immediately remembered Frasier from the accident. It took Frasier a few moments to remember Tippit as Wesley had been dazed from the impact of the collision. Frasier informed Tippit that Oswald's funeral was scheduled for the upcoming Friday. Tippit casually asked Frasier if he knew about the wrapped package on the floor of the back seat. Frasier quickly responded Oswald had told him the package contained curtain rods for Lee's rented room in Oak Cliff. Frazier added Oswald lived at the boarding house during the week. Oswald usually rode back with Frazier to Irving on Friday evenings to stay with Lee's wife and two daughters over the weekend at Ruth Paine's house.

Frazier also included Oswald and his wife Marina were having some marital problems; the underlying reason for Lee staying at the rooming house during the work week. Wesley shook his head and said it was a shame Lee had decided to come back to Irving Thursday night to get those stupid curtain rods. Otherwise he would not have been in the car last Friday morning and would still be alive. As Tippit was leaving Frazier volunteered he felt sorry for Oswald's wife Marina as she was Russian; spoke little English; and was left with 2 small children.

Tippit paused and asked Frazier if he knew how Oswald had met Marina. Frazier nonchalantly answered Oswald had met her while living in the Soviet Union. When Tippit inquired why Oswald was living there, Frazier said Oswald had vaguely explained he went there as a student. Reportedly Lee had an interest in the Russian language and decided to study there after leaving the Marine Corps. Tippit slowly nodded his head and thanked Frazier for his time.

§

Truly then took Tippit up to the sixth floor where Oswald filled book orders. It was the first time Truly had been up there since the accident and the excitement of Kennedy's motorcade the previous Friday.

Truly walked over to the southeast corner window which overlooked the intersection of Houston and Elm Streets. He appeared puzzled. The window was surrounded with boxes of books; almost like a barricade or enclave. When Tippet questioned him about this, Truly said the windows were kept clear to allow light in. It appeared someone had placed the boxes there on purpose. When Tippet asked him if this had ever happened before, Truly shook his head "No".

Tippit walked around the boxes and looked out the corner window. There was a clear, unobstructed view of Elm Street. Actually Elm Street intersected Houston at a slight diagonal angle. Thus the Kennedy motorcade had to significantly slow down to make the left turn onto Elm and drive past the Depository building. This was the last portion of the parade route as Elm provided a direct route to the Trade Mart where Kennedy later delivered his luncheon speech. As he gazed out the window Tippit's old wartime paratrooper instincts were aroused. This would have made an excellent sniper position.

Tippet thanked Truly for his cooperation. As he left the building Tippit decided he needed to talk to Detective Leavelle. Tippet called Leavelle's office and set an appointment for Tuesday afternoon.

§

Leavelle and Tippet had never met before. Leavelle was curious why Tippit was spending so much extra time on this accident case. Tippet deliberately reviewed all the points of his follow-up efforts. Though it was all speculative and circumstantial to this point, Tippit recommended a further background check of Oswald and a personal interview with Marina Oswald.

After a thoughtful pause, Leavelle agreed to perform the background check. But he was going to delay talking with Marina until after Oswald's funeral; no use getting her unnecessarily upset.

Three weeks later Tippet was contacted by Leavelle. Leavelle asked Tippit to meet with him the next afternoon after work at a local downtown bar. Leavelle stated he had some very interesting information about Oswald.

§

The following afternoon Tippit arrived at the bar at the appointed time. Leavelle was at a back booth and motioned to Tippit as he entered. After Tippit joined him,

Leavelle clarified this meeting was "off the record". Also, Tippit needed to agree to keep this conversation confidential. Leavelle was aware of Tippit's honorable war record and his respected police reputation to date. In light of this, Leavelle felt Tippit deserved to know the results of the Oswald inquiry.

Tippit readily agreed. What followed was almost beyond belief.

The personal history of Lee Harvey Oswald was very unusual, bordering on the bizarre. Oswald's childhood was a confusion of multiple moves between different residences and schools in New Orleans, New York and Dallas. He had dropped out of high school and joined the Marines at age 17; only to receive a hardship discharge to allegedly support his apparently unstable mother. After receiving the discharge Oswald made his way to the Soviet Union in 1959 and declared his intention to renounce his American citizenship. Though the Soviets were initially skeptical, Oswald was eventually allowed into the country and assigned work at an electronics factory. After being rejected by one Russian woman, he married his wife Marina. After the birth of their first daughter, Oswald requested, and received permission, to return to the United States in June, 1962. This action raised the awareness of the FBI. Upon Lee's return to Dallas, he was questioned by Special Agent James Hosty of the Dallas FBI office.

In fact, Leavelle was directly contacted by Hosty when Leavelle first inquired about Oswald through the Dallas FBI. Hosty was curious about Leavelle's interest in Oswald. After meeting with Leavelle and Dallas Detective

Captain Will Fritz, Hosty joined the current investigation of Oswald.

Hosty and Leavelle interviewed Marina Oswald the Monday after Oswald's funeral. They decided to meet Marina at Ruth Paine's house to help ease the situation. Marina appeared very nervous but was willing to cooperate with them.

Marina openly shared her account of Oswald's multifaceted activities since their emigration from the Soviet Union in June, 1962. Following their arrival in Dallas, Lee went through a series of failed jobs; first in Dallas and then in New Orleans.

Fortunately, Marina had been quickly befriended by Ruth Paine. Ruth later helped Marina move to New Orleans in April, 1963 to follow Lee. However, Lee's job results were no better in New Orleans and their marriage was suffering as well. In September 1963, Ruth moved Marina and her daughters back to Dallas to live in Ruth's house.

For unknown reasons, Lee had become involved in New Orleans with the pro-Castro group "Fair Play for Cuba". After Marina returned to Dallas, Lee travelled to Mexico City in an unsuccessful attempt to gain admission to Cuba. Oswald then returned to Dallas in October, 1963. Through Ruth Paine's acquaintance Wesley Frazier, Lee secured a job at the Texas School Book Depository. As Ron Truly verified, Lee had only worked there a month before the fatal automobile accident.

Tippit could only shake his head.

Yet, Leavelle pointed out, there was more.

Earlier in March, 1963 Oswald had purchased a 6.5 mm Carcano rifle and a .38 caliber Smith & Wesson handgun by mail-order using the alias A. Hidell. A fake ID with that alias was found in Oswald's personal effects. The .38 handgun was later found at Oswald's boarding house room in Oak Cliff.

When asked about the rifle, Marina appeared surprised and anxious; especially when the weapon was not found in Ruth Paine's garage where Lee had kept it. Marina showed Hosty and Leavelle a photograph of Lee holding both the rifle and the handgun.

Back on April 10, 1963, the Dallas police responded to a report of a shot fired at retired Major General Edwin Walker in his home in Dallas. The shot missed and struck a window frame. While the bullet was too damaged for a ballistics test, it was determined to be a 6.5 mm caliber rifle round. Marina stated Lee later told her he was the shooter.

Even more puzzling was Oswald's actions that fateful Friday morning before he left for work early with Frazier. Marina reported she did not wake up until after Lee left. When she got up, Marina discovered Lee had left his wedding ring in a small china cup, as well as $170 in cash, on the dresser in their bedroom. Marina was fairly confident this was all the money Lee had at the time. Oswald left no explanation for these actions. Marina admitted being very worried about Lee's reasons for doing this. It appeared he was planning not to return.

§

After letting all this sink in, Leavelle told Tippit that Hosty had direct orders from FBI Director J. Edgar Hoover to keep all of this information secret. The implications of Oswald possibly being an agent for either the Soviet Union or Cuba in a potential assassination attempt of President Kennedy were too dire to risk any public awareness.

Leavelle emphasized he felt Tippit deserved to know the outcome of this investigation. If not for Tippit's extra efforts, none of this would have been discovered.

Tippit solemnly nodded and thanked Leavelle for his trust.

Tippit did have one more question. What was going to happen to Jack Ruby?

Leavelle gave a wry smile.

The FBI concluded Ruby had, though quite unintentionally, prevented a potential tragedy. Jack just didn't need to know about it. Also, Marina Oswald and Wesley Frazier needed to quickly and quietly move on with their lives.

Jack Ruby was told the police could not determine whether he or Frazier had caused the accident by running a red light at the intersection. No traffic citation would be issued; no fault was assigned. Therefore, Ruby's insurance company would repair the damage to Jack's car. Likewise,

Frazier's insurance would compensate Wesley for his vehicle's damage.

Marina Oswald was informed Ruby's insurance company agreed to pay her a $20,000 settlement for the accidental death of her husband. Frazier was separately notified the replacement value of his car was paid through Ruby's insurance coverage.

The actual payments to all three of these individuals (in addition to the owner of the damaged delivery truck) were ultimately paid by the FBI.

The FBI did not want Ruby, Frazier or Marina to be involved in any further legal, financial or other public repercussions from the accident.

Besides, who would ever imagine the government would conspire to cover up the circumstances of this little known automobile accident?

§

The following week, Officer J.D. Tippit was promoted to the rank of Sergeant in the Dallas Police Department. All of his family, friends and fellow police officers felt the promotion was long overdue.

Postscript
Alternate history, sometimes called counter-factual writing, attempts to provide interesting, thoughtful versions of "What If". The two related short stories "A Day in Dallas"

and "Next Days in Dallas" are based on documented backgrounds of real life people. In writing these fictional accounts I intended no disrespect to any of the identified people, either living or deceased. In retrospect, all were tragically associated with that memorable day in November, 1963.

Remembering most conspiracy theories reflect an innate desire for emotional drama over actual circumstances. Even after over 50 years, many people find it difficult to accept that an ordinary person like Lee Harvey Oswald caused the death of an extraordinary person like John F. Kennedy.

Abel Ducked

There's a continuing debate on whether biblical stories should be taken at literal, face value; or if such stories are more complex metaphors containing subtle or hidden wisdom. I think the problem began with Genesis. For instance, if the Almighty did create the universe, world and mankind in six days, He had to do it by Himself (because even He couldn't get anyone else to work that fast before money was even invented).

If you believe the stories in the Bible are literal, then also remember these stories were about people and their ongoing relationships with each other. If this was so, then there had to be other things going on which were not written down.

For instance, there's the forbidden fruit story in the Garden of Eden. Poor Adam, he's got it made. He's got the perfect place to live. No problems getting good food. No worries about work. He's given a wife who was made to help him and to make him happy. Then the problems start. First time she can get into trouble, she does. She can have anything she wants except for two things. So what does she do?

She immediately goes after one of the two things she can't have; forgetting about everything else. She doesn't listen to the Almighty. She doesn't listen to her husband (at least she had the opportunity to be the first wife to do this). She listens to some snake (and she wouldn't be the last wife to do that). Anyway, Eve eats the forbidden fruit and then offers some to Adam.

84

Maybe her rebellion with the rules didn't happen without some justification (at least from her perspective). Even though Genesis doesn't specifically say so, I'm guessing one of the first disagreements Eve had with Adam was when it came to naming the animals.

Here's the situation. The Creator instructs (delegates) Adam to name all the animals. Not even attempting to know the Creator's reason for this, I'm thinking either He was tired from all the Creation activities; or He wanted to get Adam more involved in managing Eden. Imagine this, Adam comes home all excited about completing this naming responsibility and can't wait to tell Eve. On hearing this, Eve's first question concerns his lack of consideration in leaving her out of this process. How could he do this to her! Doesn't he respect her as a person? Is he only interested her body and not her mind?

Anyway, back to the forbidden fruit. Now Adam had a choice. He could disagree with his wife about eating the forbidden fruit; or he could risk the Creator's wrath. Setting the example for all future husbands, he follows his wife's wishes in order to maintain peace and quiet in his home (regardless of the consequences). Adam eats the forbidden fruit.

Actually I think the Almighty kind of expected this. He doesn't eliminate Adam, along with his disobeying wife Eve, and start all over again with humanity (though He did later reconsider this with Noah). He merely evicts them from their perfect world and tells them they're on their own. He doesn't even get rid of the snake Satan. The Almighty then demonstrates He has a certain type of subtle humor by making Satan also go out and continue to bother human kind.

So now Adam is in the real world. He's working hard to make ends meet. He misses the old stomping grounds but he has his beautiful wife. She continues to tell him how sorry she was for making that one bad decision back in Eden (which Eve continually blames on the snake). However, she works hard to make their home comfortable; cooks Adam good meals; and continues to provide him with the newly discovered pleasures of sex. Things are going well for the "first couple". Then Eve tells Adam about the next "first" they were going to experience; namely being the "first family". This actually comes as a surprise to both Adam and Eve (remember there were no other people to tell them about the "birds and the bees"). Anyway, after thinking about it, Adam not only accepts the upcoming addition to the family, he is actually happy about it.

Now we come to the story about Cain and Abel. During the birth of their first child Cain, Eve fully realizes her punishment of painful childbirth for the fruit indiscretion in Eden. She immediately tells Adam this birth discomfort is entirely his fault, and also to never touch her again. However, after things settle down, both Adam and Eve love their new son and decide they should have another child.

Soon adorable little Abel shows up. Cain is old enough to understand he now has competition for his parents' affection and attention. Thus, the "first sibling rivalry" is established. Cain soon discovers that though he is older, he receives less sympathy from his parents than little Abel in the increasing occurrences of brotherly disagreements. Abel's talent for gaining parental sympathy improves as time goes on. Cain soon learns to just let his little brother have his way. Cain's only reasonable chance for retribution lies in the hope his parents will bring another sibling into the world resulting in Abel getting what's coming to him.

To Cain's big disappointment no new brother or sister makes an appearance. Adam is growing increasingly disenchanted with the challenges of being a husband; a father; and a provider (remember Adam had no human father to mentor him in these realities of life). Adam finds he experiences more peace (and quiet) by focusing on his job of raising the crops and herding the sheep. As Cain grows older, he is brought into the family business. Adam is pleasantly surprised to find Cain is a quick learner and a good worker. Adam doesn't realize that a lot of Cain's energy for farming and herding comes from the frustrations he experiences from his little brother Abel.

Just as Cain is becoming proficient in helping his father, Abel becomes old enough to also help with the family business. Being the astute learner he was, Abel quickly determines herding sheep is a much easier, and a more preferable job, than raising crops. Additionally, it's a lot more fun working with the sheep dogs than with the larger, more stubborn and messy oxen. After Abel complains about this to his father, and especially to his mother, Adam decides to have Cain do the crop farming and Abel do the sheep herding. This again establishes Adam's goal of peace and quiet (at least with Eve and Abel). Even though he senses Cain's disappointment with this outcome, Adam figures Cain will be too busy with the crops to stay mad for long.

Then the contest arrives.

The Creator announces He wants both Cain and Abel to demonstrate to Him their abilities in their respective vocations in the form of an offering to Him of their best outputs.

Cain greets this opportunity with relish. Finally he'll be able to show he merits being the favored son (unlike his manipulating little brother). His long, quiet suffering is finally to be rewarded. His father and mother will finally have Abel's "wool" (bad pun) pulled from their eyes.

Cain knows just the plot of ground which will yield the best crop. He gives extra attention to it and rejoices in how the weather cooperates to deliver his best crop ever. During his work, he can't help but notice that Abel was expending no discernible extra efforts with his herds.

On the morning Cain arrives to harvest the crop from his prized plot of ground, he is greeted with the sight of Abel's sheep grazing on the crops. Actually Abel had just arrived with two of his sheep dogs to drive the sheep back to their normal grazing fields. Abel was very apologetic, stating the sheep had somehow broken through the fence. As Abel drove the sheep away, neither brother noticed a snake quietly slithering away.

Two days later, the big offering event happened. First place went to Abel; second place to Cain. (Actually Abel was about to win first and second place because he offered both a sheep and a goat. However Cain objected as he didn't know more than one offering was allowed.)

Cain was inconsolable. Adam and Eve tried to be supportive. Cain left them in a huff.

A couple days later Abel came over to see Cain. Abel immediately saw that Cain was not in a good mood. He had seen many similar moods in his brother over the years. Abel remembered when they were small children how Cain used to chase him and beat him up for being a pest. Somehow Abel always knew he probably deserved it.

This time though, there was a more menacing difference. Abel was extra alert.

Abel started the conversation by attempting to apologize for his sheep grazing on Cain's prime ground.

Something in Cain snapped, and he impulsively swung the shovel in his hands at Abel's head.

Instinctively Abel ducked; barely avoiding Cain's blow.

Losing his balance, Abel fell back into a pile of ox dung in the field.

Cain quickly recovered and was ready to swing the shovel at Abel's head again. When he saw Abel's situation, Cain dropped the shovel and began laughing.

Realizing what he had fallen into, Abel looked up at Cain; and broke into spontaneous laughter.

(From then on whenever someone was observed to accidentally step into animal droppings, it was jokingly referred to as the "Mark of Abel".)

Afterwards both of them fully grasped how lucky it was Cain missed Abel with the shovel. Cain could have killed Abel!

Then Cain would have had to put up with their future youngest brother Seth all by himself.

And everyone knows what a spoiled little devil Seth turned out to be.

Lingering

Though blind, justice sometimes demonstrates a subtle sense of humor.

Sean's thoughts always lingered when he passed this intersection. Sean felt he was making a gesture to recognize the personal value of that past event.

Maybe that's why he always drove by this place whenever he came back to his home town. The past event had prominently registered itself in Sean's memory. Maybe it was his self-imposed reminder of when he purposely made a balanced, yet just decision.

Many people would have just chalked it up as a youthful experience on the way to becoming an adult.

It was a funny thing though. Sean could always remember both of his parents repeatedly admonishing him to act like an adult. As he got older Sean could not help but notice how the so-called adults continued to act in childish ways. People would gossip about others; easily passing on rumors and unsupported speculations to other willing ears. He also noticed grown-ups, when faced with a tough choice, would invariably put themselves first; regardless of prior declarations of concern for others.

People seemed to be easily influenced by others with perceived power. The mayor's impulsive son never getting a speeding ticket. The school board members' kids always making the varsity athletic teams. The bank president's unruly daughter never having to stay after school for detention.

It was the spring of his high school senior year. Everyone in Sean's class was in the process of counting down the days to graduation. This cultural rite of passage was an assumed entitlement; fully expected and practiced by each successive senior class. With less than two weeks left before the graduation ceremony, even daily attendance was becoming an unrealistic, seemingly oppressive requirement. It was time to follow the time-honored practice of the senior "skip" day.

Past senior classes had chosen either a common class excursion or fragmented smaller group activities. Sean's class went with the smaller groups' choice. Sean thought this selection was appropriate given the variety of cliques comprising their informal high school social hierarchy system. While Sean was not a member of the elites, he also was not one of the lowly untouchables. For no specific reasons, he had always accepted the elevated social status of the elites as a given.

Mondays or Fridays were popular days to "skip" to extend a weekend. The Monday of their last week of school was so designated by popular acclaim. Sean was on the golf team. He and three classmates decided to play golf at a course in a neighboring town. This designated "skip" day fit well with their plans as Mondays were typically slack golfing days; easier to get on courses with fewer other golfers to impede their play.

Monday was a nice sunny spring day. Sean and his three friends enjoyed a leisurely round of golf. After golf they had a late lunch at the course club house. Sean's friend

Ben mentioned many of their classmates were having a "kegger" at a popular beach along the river outside of town. Ben assured the other three golfers all members of their senior class were welcome. Sean agreed it would be fun to attend. It was their last week of high school; they deserved it.

Ben drove up to the beach at sunset. Quite a few cars were already parked there. As they approached a bonfire, Sean recognized most of the attendees as fellow classmates. He could tell some of them had been there for quite a while. There were actually two large kegs of beer and the golden brew was flowing freely. A good time was being had by all.

Sometime later the other two golfers walked up to Sean. They were going to ride back to town with some other friends. Last week of school or not, tomorrow was still Tuesday. It was too early in the week for an extended hangover. After they left, Sean started looking for Ben. Sean actually heard him first. Ben was standing beside the fire, singing their high school fight song at the top of his lungs. At the end of the song he proposed a toast to the prosperous future of his fellow classmates. Luckily Sean got to Ben as he drained the last drop of his plastic cup and started to collapse towards the fire. Sean caught him and started to drag Ben back to his car.

After depositing Ben in the back seat, Sean procured the keys from Ben's pocket and assumed the driver's position. Ben was snoring contently as Sean steered the car down the beach road towards the main highway.

93

Suddenly a car appeared in back of Sean with its high beams on and passed Sean at a high rate of speed. Sean immediately recognized Burt Stone's car. Burt was class president, all state football halfback and homecoming king. Burt had also beat up Ben last fall because Ben had allegedly tried to pick up Burt's steady girlfriend at the homecoming football game. Unfortunately for Ben, Burt's girlfriend had mistakenly identified Ben instead of the real offender. Apparently Burt used up all his anger hitting Ben. When the flighty girl later made the correct identification, a stern verbal warning was all that was necessary to scare the real offender away.

Burt never even apologized to Ben; attributing the misdirected action as fair warning to any other potential interlopers. Whether out of fear of future encounters with Burt or heeding the cultural aversion of being labeled a squealer, Ben maintained his silence and quietly healed. Ben's standard response to inquiries about his injuries was he fell down the crowded football stadium seats while cheering for one of Burt's homecoming game touchdowns. Ben had a rather dry, self-deprecating sense of humor; a key attribute for one of perceived inferior social status.

As the tail lights of Burt's car rapidly melted into the night, Sean wondered if Burt would remember the upcoming stop sign at the beach road T-intersection with the main highway. As Sean started slowing down for the stop sign, he suddenly saw the brake lights of Burt's car as it barreled across the intersection, sliced through a barbed wire fence, and approached a small stand of trees. One tree engaged the front bumper causing Burt's car to abruptly halt;

94

sending Burt, unencumbered by a seat belt, into the windshield.

After stopping at the intersection and observing no other vehicles in the vicinity, Sean lingered long enough to ascertain the results of Burt's driving indiscretion. Hearing Burt groaning, Sean was confident Burt was still alive. With a new clarity of purpose, Sean left Burt's aid to others of Burt's esteemed social status. Sean drove into town well within the posted speed limit; never looking back.

Sean drove to Ben's house and parked the car in the driveway. Sean kept the car keys. He would give them back to Ben the next day at school. Sean figured it was between Ben and his parents on whether Ben would sleep in his car or in his bed that night. It was a nice cool spring evening for Sean to walk the three blocks to his home.

Next day all the school was talking about Burt going through the intersection, wrecking his car, breaking his nose and suffering assorted cuts and bruises. Almost like getting beat up.

Sean didn't know much about poetry but he quickly came to the conclusion justice had been served. He decided someday he would tell Ben what happened.

Sean's thoughts would always linger whenever he came back to his home town and passed that intersection.

"Lingering" first appeared in the Winter-Spring 2016 Edition of "The Rockford Review" published by the Rockford Writers' Guild.

Southern Spring

The members of the tribe were beginning to stir. The early morning haze was still clinging to the ground. The dew was heavy on the grass but was not frost. Spring had finally arrived after a long difficult winter. Few of the elder tribe members could remember a more severe winter.

Roland had to admit it was the hardest winter since he had assumed the role as tribal leader three years ago. The tribe had lost almost a quarter of its members including a third of its children under 10 years of age. The tribe could not continue to sustain such losses. Roland was reluctantly coming to the conclusion that they must continue to move south. Even though such movement would increase the risk of encountering other tribes with similar ideas. Past experience had shown such encounters to be perilous.

The eldest member of the tribe was an old woman named Naomi who was over 70 years old. She had surprisingly survived to this advanced age when most others rarely lived past 50. She was held in respect by the tribe and her counsel was actively sought by the tribal leaders. Roland was on his way to discuss his plans of moving south with her. He smiled to himself because Naomi was also his grandmother; and he couldn't remember a time she was not there to seek advice.

Roland asked his two lieutenants to accompany him to see Naomi. Helmut and Ricardo were not related to Roland. But they all had grown up together in the tribe and were long-time friends. Both of them valued Naomi's counsel and trusted Roland's judgment. Many lives in the tribe, including their own, had been preserved by following Roland's decisions. In fact the prior leader Jonathon had died because he chose to ignore Roland's recommendation to avoid contact with a larger tribe. Though Jonathon valiantly died in delaying an attack by this aggressive tribe, allowing most of the tribe to safely escape, most felt his death was a tragic waste.

Roland as the senior lieutenant was chosen to succeed Jonathon as tribal leader by popular acclaim. He reluctantly accepted; fully realizing the awesome responsibility of the position.

Naomi observed Roland, Helmut and Ricardo approaching. She instructed the other family members around their camp fire to pack up and leave her alone with the approaching leaders.

Roland came up to the fire, "Good morning Grandmother."

Naomi nodded to the three, "A nice spring morning Grandson."

Roland somberly responded, "We have come for counsel."

Naomi gestured to them, "Please sit down by the fire. I was half expecting you."

The four of them talked for over an hour.

Naomi reaffirmed the winters were continuing to worsen. This trend had continued since the time of her grandmother; even though the tribe had continued to gradually move south trying to stay ahead of the advancing cold. Her grandmother had reminisced about earlier times when winters were shorter and the tribe had a permanent settlement and engaged in growing food crops.

Relationships with other tribes were of a peaceful nature reinforced by trading goods.

However as the creeping cold forced the different tribes south, competition for increasing scarce resources caused such tribal relationships to become adversarial. Tribes adopted more migratory survival strategies and became more reliant on hunting and gathering for sustenance.

Yet there were persistent tales of warmer climates to the south. Places which never experienced the snow and cold of winter. The trade-off was all the competing tribes told the same tales. The mythical southern Promised Land was a common hope. A hope which carried a real parallel risk to the tribe's survival.

Naomi remembered her grandmother had talked about a "Land of Flowers" where in the past people would travel for rest and relaxation. Naomi had to further explain the meaning of relaxation to Roland and his lieutenants. They could only laugh and shake their heads. Even though they respected Naomi, they thought she was getting a little daft in her old age. Still there must be some truth in this ongoing myth. Regardless, it couldn't be any worse further south than it was at their present location.

After the conversation with Naomi, Roland reviewed all the factors with Helmut and Ricardo. They agreed with his decision to use this spring and summer to move as far south as possible.

They would break with their tradition of gradually moving with the seasons and instead make a forced march to find a warmer, more hospitable climate.

Roland was betting the survival of the tribe on this spring-initiated migration.

Naomi remembered her grandmother had indicated the mythical "Land of Flowers" was a long distance away. Roland estimated the tribe could walk an average of five miles a day while remaining together for group security and foraging enough food for their survival. They would be dependent upon their advance scouts to identify passable trails; find suitable food and water resources; and avoid other aggressive tribes. Roland fully expected they would encounter more tribes with similar plans the further south they traveled.

At this rate of travel the group should be able to travel some 900 miles over 6 months' time. At that point they would have to establish a camp with suitable shelter and foodstuffs for the winter. Roland was uncertain as to the chances for the tribes' survival if a more habitable environment was not found. Yet he was convinced they would be better off leaving than if they remained in their current situation.

During their past wanderings, they had come across stretches of strange trails made of hard, stone-like materials that were for the most part broken into irregular segments. As they progressed south, these trails were more intact. However, the scouts were finding more and more other tribes following these trails. The tribe became very proficient in quickly abandoning these trails when their scouts warned them of another approaching tribe.

On two occasions the warriors and scouts had to defend the main body of the tribe from surprise attacks by other aggressive tribes following similar paths. Luckily causalities from both encounters were light. It seemed other tribes simply wanted to be left alone.

Another benefit of advancing further south was the amount of game and edible plants increased. Thus foraging for food became an easier task and the pace of the tribe's trek doggedly accelerated.

There was little evidence of the past encroaching cold. Nights were warmer than the comparable experience of the northern seasons. The spirits of the tribe were improving. A definite transition from cautious hope to confident mutual assurance.

Some six months into the journey Roland decided to have a tribal meeting. While there were still many uncertainties facing the tribe, he felt it was an appropriate time to take stock of their situation. All the members of the tribe were gathered together except for the perimeter guards.

Roland began the meeting by congratulating every tribal member on working together to achieve their successful journey to date. Now was the time to decide what next steps the tribe needed to take.

There was a long silence.

Finally Naomi stood up and proclaimed, "We will follow your leadership and trust in your decisions."

The rest of the tribe loudly cheered their agreement.

One week later the tribe was following an intact stretch of a rock hard trail. Along the side of the wide path was a large, flat, upright wooden structure. Around the perimeter were faded paintings of flowers. Most of the flat surface was covered with the faded, unfamiliar symbols "Welcome to Florida".

Roland brought Naomi up to view this strange structure. "Grandmother, what does this mean?"

Naomi looked at it for a while, "I think we have arrived in the 'Land of Flowers'."

About the Author

Alan Youmans lives with his wife Julene in Freeport, Illinois. He was born in Nebraska; grew up in Iowa; and worked in Illinois and Wisconsin. He has a BS in Psychology from Dana College and an MBA from the University of Iowa.

Besides his attempts at writing, Al likes to read, chase golf balls around golf courses, dabble in cooking, and travel about.

As a recipient of this collection, Al appreciates the time you're taking to read these words. Hopefully you'll find some enjoyment and insights in the subjects. If you also read any of his other publications, he thanks you for your ongoing support.

§

You can reach Al through the following e-mail address:
ayoumans17@gmail.com

Other Books by the Author:

An Anthology of Whimsical Writings ©2012
(Collection of Short Stories)

A Rambling Assortment of Writings ©2013
(Collection of Short Stories)

The 24242 Word Medley ©2015
(Collection of Short Stories)

Expansion: Space Travel o'er Time ©2016
(Science Fiction Novel)

www.ingramcontent.com/pod-product-compliance
Lightning Source LLC
Chambersburg PA
CBHW071326310526
45789CB00016B/935